TED SAUC

Bottoms Up

WITH ILLUSTRATIONS BY TWELVE OF

AMERICA'S MOST DISTINGUISHED ARTISTS

ARTHUR WILLIAM BROWN

GILBERT BUNDY

ROBERT BUSHNELL

EARL CORDREY

BRADSHAW CRANDELL

PHIL DORMONT

AL DORNE

JOHN FALTER

JAMES MONTGOMERY FLAGG

JOHN LA GATTA

RUSSELL PATTERSON

BEN STAHL

DECORATIONS BY RUSSELL PATTERSON

COVER DESIGN BY AL DORNE

Martino Publishing
Mansfield Centre, CT
2011

Martino Publishing
P.O. Box 373,
Mansfield Centre, CT 06250 USA

ISBN 1-891396-65-X

© 2011 Martino Publishing

Cover design by T. Matarazzo

Printed in the United States of America On 100% Acid-Free Paper

TED SAUCIER'S

Bottoms Up

WITH ILLUSTRATIONS BY TWELVE OF

AMERICA'S MOST DISTINGUISHED ARTISTS

ARTHUR WILLIAM BROWN

GILBERT BUNDY

ROBERT BUSHNELL

EARL CORDREY

BRADSHAW CRANDELL

PHIL DORMONT

AL DORNE

JOHN FALTER

JAMES MONTGOMERY FLAGG

JOHN LA GATTA

RUSSELL PATTERSON

BEN STAHL

DECORATIONS BY RUSSELL PATTERSON

COVER DESIGN BY AL DORNE

GREYSTONE PRESS, NEW YORK

DEDICATED TO

Ruth

MY LOVELY WIFE,

MY SEVEREST CRITIC,

AND

MY GREATEST HELPMATE

Contents

Illustrations

National Toasts

AMERICAN	*Bottoms Up*		GREEK	*Is Yghian*
	Here's to Your		HAWAIIAN	*Hauoli Maoli Oe*
	Good Health		HEBREW	*Lehayim*
	Here's How		HUNGARIAN	*Kedves Ejeszsejera*
	Happy Days		IRISH	*Slainte*
ARGENTINIAN	*Salud*		ITALIAN	*A la Salute*
AUSTRALIAN	*Cheers*		JAPANESE	*Banzai*
AUSTRIAN	*Prost*		MEXICAN	*Salud*
BELGIAN	*À Votre Santé*		NORWEGIAN	*Skaal*
BOHEMIAN	*Na Zdar*		PALESTINIAN	*Lehayim*
BRAZILIAN	*Viva*		PANAMANIAN	*Salud*
CANADIAN	*Happy Days*		POLISH	*Na Zdrowie*
CHILIAN	*Salud*		PORTUGUESE	*À Vossa Saude*
CHINESE	*Kong Chien*		ROMANIAN	*Noroc*
CUBAN	*Salud*		RUSSIAN	*Za Vacha Zdorovye*
DANISH	*Skål*		SCOTCH	*Here's tae Ye*
DUTCH	*Gezondheid*		SPANISH	*Salud*
EGYPTIAN	*Fi-Sihatdak*		SWEDISH	*Skål*
ENGLISH	*Cheerio*		SWISS	*À Votre Santé*
FINNISH	*Kippis*			*Prosit*
FRENCH	*À Votre Santé*		TURKISH	*Serefinize*
GERMAN	*Prosit*			

Evoe!

EVOE! —*Cry of the Bacchanals (cry of exhilaration at the feast of Bacchus, the pagan god of wine, drink, and merrymaking)*

Bar Measures

1 BAR GLASS	1½ oz.
1 BARSPOON	⅛ oz.
1 CUP	8 oz.
1 DASH	⅙ teaspoon
1 FIFTH	25.6 oz.
1 JIGGER	1½ oz. (equal to a small whisky or bar glass)
1 PINT	16 oz.
1 PONY	1 oz.
1 QUART	32 oz.
1 SPLIT	6 oz. (or ½ regular-sized bottle of carbonated water)
1 TEASPOON	⅛ oz.
1 WINE GLASS	4 oz.

Tippling Tips

For perfect results in mixing drinks, follow instructions accurately. Correct measurements are essential, as are ingredients, in following a specific recipe, or else you'll have to give the drink a new name. Comply with methods of procedure to the letter and in order given. *Stir,* when so instructed. *Shake,* when the recipe calls for shaking. Do not use *drops* when it says *dashes.*

Ingredients mix more readily in a shaker larger than the quantity of the mixture, and the shaker should be shaken as hard as possible.

When a recipe calls for sour fruit juice (lemon or lime), it should be put into the mixing glass with the required sugar or other sweetener before any liquor is added. Honey also should be dissolved with fruit juice before other ingredients are added.

All ice—cubed, cracked or shaved—must be pure, crystal-clear, hard-frozen and taste-free. A good drink can be spoiled by poor ice, for ice, while being frozen, readily absorbs foreign odors, if exposed to them. Such ice, in melting, contaminates the taste of the drink. Ice should be put into a drink first, not only to chill each ingredient thoroughly as added, but also to avoid splashing and spilling.

Remember that ice melts and that too much stirring of a drink dilutes it. On the other hand, too little stirring does not mix the ingredients properly and fails to chill the ingredients. Never stir carbonated water with too much vigor, or release of the carbonic gas will result in a drink that is flat.

Correct glassware is essential for perfect drinks and it should be more than just clean; it should sparkle. Use of two towels for glassware is advisable—one for drying, the other for polishing.

Chill cocktail glasses before pouring in the drink.

Don't let a cocktail stand too long. Drink it as soon as possible, while it is "alive."

When a recipe requires frosting the rim of a glass, moisten the rim lightly, then dip it into powdered sugar.

Palatable sparkling water is a "must" for a pleasing drink. A flat drink has no life or zest. Carbonated water, charged water or club soda can be used, regardless of which is called for in a recipe, since they are practically the same. But quality water is essential, for poor water will kill fine whisky, gin or brandy.

Simple sirup, which mixes instantly, can be used in place of sugar (lump, granulated or powdered), which is difficult to dissolve in alcohol. It also makes a smoother drink of richer taste. Using a 1-gallon enamel or aluminum vessel, add 2 quarts of water to 8 pounds of granulated sugar. Stir thoroughly occasionally, and gradually add sufficient water to make 1 gallon of sirup. Fill convenient-sized bottles and store in a cool place for use as desired.

Bitters, expertly used, give fragrance and flavor to a cocktail, which both quicken and satisfy the senses. Only two varieties of bitters—flavoring and aromatic—should be used in mixed drinks, but one must not be substituted for another. Orange, lemon and lime bitters are important flavorings, especially when a fragrant aroma is desired. Aromatic bitters are essential to correct mixing of a larger variety of drinks than flavoring bitters, due to the fact that cocktails are primarily appetizers and that aromatic bitters have an appetite-stimulating effect.

Glossary of Drinks

COBBLER   A summer drink made of iced wine or spirits and sugar, served in a wine goblet and decorated with fresh fruit after the ingredients are mixed.

COLLINS   A tall iced drink of spirits, sugar, and lime or lemon juice, served in a 14-oz. glass.

COOLER   A tall refreshing drink of Boston origin—juice ½ lemon, ¼ teaspoon sugar, 1 jigger spirits, ice, and soda water, served in Collins glass.

CUP   A beverage made of wine, usually iced, with flavoring herbs and fruits, and served in garnished pitchers, to be poured at the table.

FIZZ   An effervescing drink usually made of juice ½ lemon, ½ teaspoon sugar, fruit sirups, spirits, ice and charged water.

FLIP   A drink made with liquor and sugar, mixed with an egg, and spiced.

FRAPPÉ   An after-dinner drink of liqueur served in a cocktail glass over shaved ice.

HIGHBALL   A tall drink, served in a large highball glass, consisting of 1 jigger of a specified spirit, cracked ice and charged water.

JULEP   A mixed drink featuring fresh mint, bourbon or rye whisky, and chipped or crushed ice, served in a frosted glass.

PUNCH A drink usually mixed in a bowl in large quantity and served from the buffet in cups or glasses. A punch may also be mixed and served in individual glasses. Care should be taken to mix ingredients in such a way that neither the sweet, the bitter, the spirits or any other liquor is more apparent than another.

RICKEY A drink made of a specified spirit, served in a tumbler or tall glass with the juice and rind of half a lime, ice and charged water.

SANGAREE A drink made of wine and sugar served in a small bar glass with ice and topped with grated nutmeg; or red wine and water, spiced and sugared.

SETUP All the makings for a specified drink except the spirits.

SLING A drink of brandy, whisky or gin, with sugar and nutmeg.

SMASH A drink made of liquor and mint, water, sugar and ice—a miniature julep.

SOUR A spirituous beverage requiring lemon or lime juice, and sugar.

SWIZZLE A drink made by putting ingredients into a glass pitcher with plenty of shaved ice and agitating vigorously with a swizzle stick between the palms of the hands until the pitcher frosts. Or, a cocktail shaker may be used, if you haven't a swizzle stick with its radiating forked branch ends.

TODDY A drink made of spirits, sugar and water. Generally hot water is used and other ingredients.

The Correct Glassware

Photographs on the following two pages
picture the glasses in general use today for
the serving of cocktails, wines and spirits

The Correct Glassware

LEFT-HAND PAGE

TOP ROW
Left to right: Beer Mug; Pilsner Beer Glass; Beer Goblet; Old-Fashioned Glass; Cocktail Glass.

MIDDLE ROW
8-oz. Goblet; 8-oz. Tumbler; 8-oz. Fizz, Delmonico or Lemonade Glass; 12-oz. John Collins Glass; 14-oz. Tom Collins Glass.

BOTTOM ROW
1½-oz. Whisky or Bar Glass; 8-oz. Highball Glass; 10-oz. Highball Glass; 12-oz. Highball Glass.

ABOVE

TOP ROW
Hollow-stemmed Sparkling Burgundy Glass; Hock or Rhine Wine Glass; Sherry Glass; Port Glass; Sauterne Glass; Claret Glass; Still Burgundy Glass.

BOTTOM ROW
Saucer Champagne Glass; Hollow-stemmed Champagne Glass; Goblet Champagne Glass; Small, Tulip-Shaped Brandy Snifter; Large, Tulip-Shaped Brandy Snifter; 3-oz. Frappé Glass; Liqueur Glass; Brandy Pony or Pousse-Café Glass.

Wining and Dining

By CLAUDE C. PHILLIPE,

Of The Waldorf-Astoria,
World-Famous Host
and Leading Authority on Wines and Food

The rules governing the service of wines with food are very simple—dry white wines are preferably served with fish, red wines with meat or roast courses. At a simple dinner, it is customary to serve a single beverage throughout the dinner, and if this is the case, the wine selected for the main course is used: a dry white wine, if your course is a fish dish; or a red wine (claret preferably), if you are serving a roast. If the course is game (such as pheasant, partridge, or wild duck), a fine still Burgundy is selected.

White wines are cooled before use, and all red still wines are served at room temperature. Sparkling wines, such as sparkling Burgundy and champagne, are served well chilled.

WITH THE FIRST COURSE (oysters, clams, sea food, etc.), the following white wines are recommended:

A dry white Bordeaux, such as a Graves, preferably château-bottled (bottled at the château and sold under the name of the château), as Château Haut-Brion Blanc 1947, and white Burgundies, such as Chablis, Pouilly Fuisse, Meursault, Puligny-Montrachet, Chassagne-Montrachet, Montrachet.

It is preferable to select Burgundies that are bottled by the grower, known as estate bottlings, where, in addition to the township or district,

17 : *Wining and Dining*

a label also shows the vineyard, the vintage year, and the name of the grower who bottled the wine. For instance, Chablis Les Preuses 1949, Chablis Blanchots, Chablis Vaudesir or Chablis Vaillon are preferable to a bottle simply marked "Chablis."

The Meursault Perrieres of the Perrieres Vineyard, which is the finest in the Township of Meursault, is preferable to a wine simply marked "Meursault."

One can also serve with oysters, clams and sea food a dry Alsatian wine, Riesling, Gewuerz-Traminer or any of the dry Rhine and Moselle wines of Germany.

Since the repeal of prohibition, California and a few other states have produced some exceptional wines, which, though not in the same class as the great French wines, are still eminently satisfactory. Among them I would recommend Pinot Blanc, Folle Blanche, White Pinot and Beaulieu Chablis.

As a Moselle or Rhine wine type, to be recommended are Beauclair, Wente's Grey Riesling and Martini's Johannisberg Riesling. Also the fine E & K Rhine wine from Sandusky, Ohio, and the Lake Erie Valley Rhine wine from Silverton, Ohio, and two very good New York State Rhine wine types, Widmer's Lake Delaware and Lake Elvira Rhine wine from Naples.

WITH THE SOUP COURSE, the following dry sherries are recommended:

A Fino or an Amontillado of any reputable firm (a Fino is the driest; the Amontillado, although dry, has a fuller and nutty taste).

Berry Brothers, Harvey, Pedro-Domecq, Sandeman, Bobadilla and Gonzalez, Byass are all reputable firms with excellent sherries.

There are now also a number of California sherries which are well worth tasting, even in comparison with the great Spanish sherries. Notable among them are Beaulieu pale dry and the Beringer's Private Stock sherry. We should not forget the Pleasant Valley pale dry sherry from Rheims.

WITH THE FISH COURSE, the white wines recommended are the same as those outlined above for oysters and sea food; or you may serve a more full-bodied white Rhone wine, such as a Hermitage or a dry Moselle or Rhine wine.

A sweet wine should never be served with fish, as it dulls the palate and masks the flavor of the fish.

Nothing can be more horrifying than a great sauterne, such as Château d'Yquem, being served with lobster Newburg or a filet of sole *bonne femme*.

With a cold fish, particularly in the summer, one can drink any of the many agreeable light, dry *rosé* wines, which are now available from France.

There are a number of American dry sauternes which are to be recommended if served well chilled: Wente's Sauvignon Blanc, Lake Niagara dry sauterne (New York State), California dry Semillon and Fountaingrove's dry sauterne.

Pleasant in the summer particularly, with a cold fish, though also very enjoyable all year round, are a number of notable California *rosés*: the Almaden *rosé*, made from the Grenache grape which produces France's famous Tavel *rosé*; Beaulieu Beaurosé, Wente's *rosé* and Martini's Napa Gamay *rosé*.

WITH THE ROAST. With poultry, though a claret or light Burgundy is preferable, there is no objection to a light, dry white Burgundy or an agreeable chilled *rosé*.

With meat, beef, lamb, veal, a red wine is recommended. Especially appropriate is a red Bordeaux from Médoc (Margaux, St. Estephe, Pauillac) or St. Emilion. Château-bottled wines are preferable to regional wines (those sold under their regional names), and the complete list of the château-bottled wines of Médoc consists of sixty-one châteaux, divided into five growths of which the first four are Château Lafite, Château Margaux, Château Latour, and Château Haut-Brion (from the adjoining district of Graves).

The lesser the wine, the faster it matures. The greater the wine, the slower it matures. A red wine should be a minimum of three to four years old and up to twenty to thirty years sometimes for the great clarets.

The great year of 1945 (the first post-war year), is already represented in our cellars by:

> Château Beychevelle
> Château Pichon Longueville Lelande
> Château Ausone
> Château Haut-Brion
> Château Lafite
> Château Margaux
> Château Mouton-Rothschild
> Château Latour

A red Burgundy, preferably estate-bottled, is also recommended, and could be a Beaujolais (small and light) or any of the royal family of the wines of Burgundy:

The King: Le Chambertin
The Queen: La Romanée-Conti
The Royal Heir: Le Musigny

19 : *Wining and Dining*

The Royal Children: Le Richebourg, Le Clos de Vougeot, Le Corton, Le Montrachet

The Princes of the Royal Blood: Les Romanées, Le Clos de Tart, Les Echezeaux, Les Bonnes-Mares, Le Clos des Lambrays

Dukes and Duchesses: Gevrey-Chambertin, Chambolle-Musigny, Vougeot, Vosne-Romanée, Nuits-St.-Georges, Aloxe-Corton, Beaune, Pommard, Volnay, Meursault, Puligny-Montrachet, Chassagne-Montrachet

WITH GAME, PHEASANT, WILD DUCK, PARTRIDGE, ETC., any of the Burgundies or the château-bottled clarets listed above would be excellent.

In the opinion of a great many connoisseurs and European experts, America's contribution to good wines has been particularly notable among its great California red wines—Beaulieu, Georges de Latour Private Reserve cabernet, Paul Masson Pinot Noir, the Inglenook and Martini cabernets, Wente's Livermore Mourestel, Beaulieu Beaumont, Fountaingrove's Pinot Noir.

Of the above, the Burgundy types are most suitable for meats and games; with poultry, the cabernets of the claret type are most suitable.

WITH SALAD, no wines should be served, except possibly a light *rosé* or champagne.

The domestic *rosés* previously mentioned are all agreeable with salads, particularly in the summertime, when very often in this country a *salade composée* is the main course for either luncheon or dinner.

Among a fine array of domestic champagnes, Paul Masson, Korbel, Almaden from California, and Bellows from Sandusky, Ohio, are truly outstanding, together with the Charles Fournier, Cazanove Cuvée AA and Vintners champagnes from New York State.

WITH CHEESE, a good red wine. Cheese is the greatest friend of wine and, in any dinner where more than one wine is being served, one starts with the lesser-bodied wines and builds up to the great one served with the cheese.

With the many excellent domestic red wines to choose from, you will never err if you start with a cabernet, and end up serving a rich, full-bodied Burgundy type, such as Beaulieu Beaumont, with the cheese.

WITH DESSERT, a sweet wine, a sauterne, preferably château-bottled: Château d'Yquem, Château Lafite, Château Coutet, Château Climens, or a sweet Vouvray or Anjou.

A number of excellent American sweet sauternes are now on the market—from California, Château Beaulieu, a luscious wine of the Château d'Yquem type, Concannon Haut Sauterne, Inglenook Semillon and the

Château Novitiate from the Novitiate of Los Gatos. But let us not forget Wente's sweet Semillon, and from Naples, New York, Lake Niagara sauterne. These are all recommended as dessert wines, as is Los Gatos Muscat de Frontignan, which is both delicate and rich.

WITH FRUIT Cockburn, Dow's, Feuerheerd, Gonzalez, Byass, Harvey's or Sandeman port or a dry champagne, which incidentally, of course, can be served throughout luncheon or dinner.

Our American port wines are gaining many friends every year. Among the most popular of these wines are Beringer's, Christian Brothers ruby port, the Novitiate of Los Gatos black muscat, all from California. Widmer's tawny port and the Pleasant Valley white port from New York State, and Meier's tawny port from Silverton, Ohio, are also enjoyed by many.

The excellent domestic champagnes previously mentioned are of course most satisfactory wines to serve with fruit.

Wine rules are not a question of etiquette but of common sense. Just as one would start a meal with the hors d'oeuvres and finish with dessert, so one would, in serving wines, start with the dry white wine and finish with the sweet one.

When cream sauces are served, dry white wines are preferable to red ones.

Wine should be served in combination with food, the best wine being the one that pleases the palate the most. Heavy foods demand heavy wines—light foods, light wines. Large glasses are a must, as the greater the wine the more condensed is the bouquet, and a large glass helps to bring out the bouquet of any wine.

Vintage Chart

〜〜•〜〜

	RED BORDEAUX	WHITE BORDEAUX	RED BURGUNDY	WHITE BURGUNDY	CHAMPAGNE	RHINE & MOSELLE
1926	6	7	5	6	9	3
1927	0	2	0	2	0	4
1928	8½	8	7	9	10	1
1929	10	9	10	10	7	7
1930	0	0	0	0	1	1
1931	2	1	3	4	1	4
1932	0	0	1	3	4	3
1933	6½	5	6	7	9	7
1934	9	8	10	10	8	9
1935	4	4	6	8	7	7
1936	5	5	3	4	2	2
1937	9	9	8	9	8	9
1938	6	6	6	5	3	4
1939	4	5	2	2	2	2
1940	6	6	5	5½	1	3
1941	2	1	3	3	6½	4
1942	6	7	7	7	8	6
1943	9	8	9	9	9	8
1944	5	7	7	5	6	5
1945	10	10	10	10	9	9
1946	5	5	6	7½	6	7
1947	9	10	10	10	10	10
1948	7	7	7	7½	5	7
1949	9	9	10	9	8	10

〜〜•〜〜

9-10 *Very Great*   6-7-8 *Good*   4-5 *Fair*   2-3 *Poor*   0-1 *Very Poor*

Courtesy THE WALDORF-ASTORIA

Here's to the maiden of bashful fifteen;
Here's to the widow of fifty;
Here's to the flaunting, extravagant quean,
And here's to the housewife that's thrifty!
Let the toast pass;
Drink to the lass;
I'll warrant she'll prove an excuse for the glass.

RICHARD BRINSLEY SHERIDAN
(*The School for Scandal*)

ABEL GREEN SUMMER DRINK
By Abel Green, Editor, Variety, New York City

⅓ Pimm's No. 1 cup
⅓ Italian vermouth
⅓ Rhine wine
Ice

*Pour ingredients into glass-bottomed pewter mug.
Fill with ginger ale.*

ABSINTHE

2 dashes dry gin
⅔ jigger absinthe (or substitute)
⅓ jigger water
Ice

Stir. Strain into cocktail glass.

ABSINTHE DRIP

1 cube sugar
1 liqueur glass (1 oz.) absinthe

*Place sugar in bottom of drip glass. Fill drip saucer
with ice and pour the absinthe over it. Let drip
for a few minutes. Then fill glass with water over
ice in drip saucer.*

ABSINTHE FRAPPÉ
Courtesy, Old Absinthe House, New Orleans

1 teaspoon simple sirup
1 oz. plain water
1½ oz. Herbsaint (absinthe substitute)

Frappé in 8-oz. glass and serve.

ABSINTHE FRAPPÉ (variation)

1½ oz. absinthe substitute
½ oz. anisette
3 dashes Angostura bitters

*Shake thoroughly with shaved ice until shaker is
frosted. Strain into cocktail glass.*

ACADEMY AWARD

By Harrison Carroll, Motion Picture Columnist, Los Angeles Herald and Express, and Central Press

Juice ¼ lemon
Juice ¼ orange
1 jigger Schenley Reserve whisky
1 teaspoon grenadine
Ice

Shake well, and strain into cocktail glass.

ALEXANDER (brandy)

⅓ jigger brandy
⅓ jigger crème de cacao
⅓ jigger heavy cream
Ice

Shake well. Strain into cocktail glass.

ALEXANDER (gin)

⅓ jigger gin
⅓ jigger crème de cacao
⅓ jigger heavy cream
Ice

Shake well. Strain into cocktail glass.

ALFONSO XIII

Courtesy, Hotel Ritz, Paris

½ Dubonnet
½ dry sherry
Ice

Stir. Strain into cocktail glass.

ALGONQUIN

Courtesy, Hotel Algonquin, New York City

1½ jiggers light rum
1 jigger blackberry brandy
¾ jigger benedictine
Juice 1 lime

Shake with shaved ice. Strain into cocktail glass.

25 : *Cocktails and Mixed Drinks*

ALICE HUGHES' A WOMAN'S NEW YORK (nonalcoholic cooler)
By Alice Hughes, Columnist, King Features Syndicate

Juice ½ orange
Juice ¼ lemon
2 barspoons grenadine
1 split (4½ oz.) grape juice

Place shaved ice in a highball glass and pour mixture over it. Fill with club soda. Serve with straws.

ALOUETTE
Courtesy, Ritz-Carlton Hotel, Montreal

2 parts rum
1 part gin
1 oz. grapefruit juice
Dash bitters
Ice

Shake well and strain into cocktail glass.

ALPINE JERICHO
Courtesy, The Alpine, Quebec

¼ oz. lime juice
¼ oz. maraschino liqueur
1¼ oz. Myers rum
Ice

Shake well and serve in 3-oz. cocktail glass.

AMBASSADOR
Courtesy, The Ambassador, Los Angeles

½ jigger brandy
¼ jigger curaçao
1 teaspoon grenadine
½ egg white
Ice

Shake well and serve in cocktail glass.

American Beauty

By JAMES MONTGOMERY FLAGG

½ oz. brandy
½ oz. dry vermouth
½ oz. grenadine
½ oz. orange juice
Dash white crème de menthe

Shake well with cracked ice, and strain into cocktail glass.

AMBASSADOR'S MORNING LIFT

Courtesy, Ambassador East, Chicago

> 1 jigger cognac (or bourbon)
> ½ jigger Jamaica rum
> ½ jigger crème de cacao
> 1 whole egg
> 1 teaspoon sugar
> 6 oz. milk
> Ice
>
> *Shake well, strain into 12-oz. glass. Top with grated nutmeg.*

AMBROSIA

Courtesy, Arnaud's Restaurant, New Orleans

(In mythology, ambrosia was the food of the gods.)

> ⅓ Italian vermouth
> ⅓ French vermouth
> ⅓ applejack
> 1 teaspoon lime juice
> Ice
> *No sugar*
>
> *Shake. Strain ingredients into champagne glass until it is half-full. Fill glass with champagne. Add a few drops of curaçao and drop in a piece of lemon peel.*

AMER PICON

> 1 oz. Amer Picon
> 1 oz. dry gin
> ¾ oz. Italian vermouth
> Dash DuBouchett caraçao
> Ice
>
> *Stir well, and strain into cocktail glass.*

27 : *Cocktails and Mixed Drinks*

ANDALUCIA FIZZ

By J. S. Brucart, Bartender, Palace Hotel, Madrid

1 cocktail glass dry sherry
Juice 1 orange
1 teaspoon sugar
Ice

Shake well, and strain into fizz glass. Fill balance of glass with soda water.

ANGEL'S TIT

(This was one of the most popular preprohibition after-dinner drinks.)

⅔ maraschino liqueur
⅓ heavy cream

Pour liqueur into a pony glass. Then pour in cream carefully, on edge of glass, so it will float and not mix with the liqueur. Top cream with maraschino cherry.

ANTOINE'S SMILE

Courtesy, Antoine's, New Orleans

1 jigger apple brandy
Juice ½ lime
1 tablespoon grenadine sirup

Shake well with cracked ice. Prepare cocktail glass by rubbing slice of lemon around rim, then dipping rim in powdered sugar. Pour cocktail into glass, twist a piece of lemon peel over it, letting it float on top.

APPLE BLOSSOM

By Paul Denis, Columnist, New York Daily Compass

(". . . guaranteed to make you feel nice without doubling your vision.")

1 dash lemon juice
1 dash Cointreau
1 jigger apple brandy
Ice

Shake well and strain into cocktail glass.

APPLEJACK

Courtesy, Sloppy Joe's Bar, Havana

1 glass applejack
1 teaspoon sugar
Juice ½ lime
A few drops DuBouchett curaçao

Shake with cracked ice and serve in cocktail glass.

APPLEJACK COLLINS

Juice ½ lemon
½ barspoon powdered sugar
1 jigger applejack

Shake well and strain into Collins glass. Add lump ice and fill glass with soda water.

APPLEJACK DAISY

Juice ½ lemon
½ teaspoon powdered sugar
6 dashes grenadine
1 jigger applejack

Half fill a highball glass with finely cracked ice. Stir until glass is frosted. Pour ingredients over ice. Fill with soda water. Decorate with sprig of fresh mint, a slice of lemon, and a slice of orange.

APPLEJACK FLIP

1 jigger applejack
½ teaspoon of sugar
1 whole egg
Ice

Shake, strain into goblet. Grate nutmeg on top.

APPLEJACK OLD-FASHIONED

1 cube sugar
1 dash Angostura bitters
1½ oz. applejack

Muddle sugar and bitters in an old-fashioned glass with a dash of soda water. Add cracked ice, apple-jack and a twist of lemon peel. Stir.

APPLEJACK ON THE ROCKS

1 jigger applejack

Fill an old-fashioned glass with cracked ice. Pour applejack over ice, add a dash of water or charged water. Also, if desired, a twist of lemon peel.

APPLEJACK RICKEY

Juice and rind ½ lime
1 jigger applejack

Place lump of ice in Delmonico glass, and pour ingredients over it. Fill with soda water.

APPLEJACK SLING

1 lump sugar dissolved in 1 teaspoon water
1 jigger applejack
1 piece twisted lemon peel

Add lump of ice and stir. Serve in whisky glass with small spoon. Top with grated nutmeg.

APPLEJACK SMASH

1 jigger applejack
2 teaspoons water
½ teaspoon sugar
3 sprigs fresh mint

Muddle sugar and water in an old-fashioned glass, with mint. Add applejack, cracked ice. Serve with small spoon.

APPLEJACK SOUR

Juice ½ lemon
½ barspoon powdered sugar
1 jigger applejack
Ice

Shake well. Strain into Delmonico glass. Add dash of club soda, half a slice of orange, and a cherry.

APPLEJACK TODDY

1 lump sugar
3 teaspoons water
1 jigger applejack

Put the sugar in an old-fashioned glass, and dissolve in the water. Add applejack, lump of ice, dash of nutmeg. Serve with a teaspoon. For a hot apple toddy, leave out the ice and add hot water.

ARISTOCRAT

Courtesy, The Colony Restaurant, New York City

2 oz. white Cuban rum
2 teaspoons cocoanut frost powder

Add small scoop of shaved ice and mix in mixer for three minutes. Serve in champagne coupe.

ARNAUD'S

Courtesy, Arnaud's Restaurant, New Orleans

⅔ Scotch
⅓ Dubonnet
Dash orange bitters
Lemon peel
Ice

Shake. Serve in a cocktail glass.

ARNAUD'S ATOMIC BOMB

Courtesy, Arnaud's Restaurant, New Orleans

⅓ gin
⅓ bottled-in-bond bourbon whisky
⅓ Italian vermouth
Dash Abbott's bitters
Ice

Shake. Serve in cocktail glass.

ARNAUD'S FRENCH 75

Courtesy, Arnaud's Restaurant, New Orleans

⅓ Italian vermouth
⅓ French vermouth
⅓ gin
1 teaspoon lime juice
Ice
No sugar.

Shake. Strain ingredients into champagne glass until half-full. Fill glass with champagne. Add a few drops of benedictine and a piece of lemon peel.

ARTHUR HALE (No. 1)

By Arthur Hale, New York City

2 parts Bacardi
1 part lime juice
½ teaspoon sugar
Dash crème de menthe
Dash Cointreau
Ice

Shake well. Strain into cocktail glass.

ARTHUR HALE (No. 2)

By Arthur Hale, New York City

2 parts bourbon
½ part (plus) Italian vermouth
½ part (minus) French vermouth
Dash benedictine
Ice

Shake. Strain into cocktail glass.

32 : *Bottoms Up*

ASTOR

Courtesy, Hotel Astor, New York City

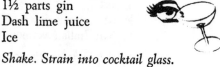

1 part Swedish punch
1½ parts gin
Dash lime juice
Ice

Shake. Strain into cocktail glass.

ASTORIA

As prepared at the old Waldorf-Astoria

2 dashes Abbott's orange bitters
⅓ Old Tom gin
⅔ French vermouth
Ice

Stir. Strain into cocktail glass.

ATOMIC BOMB

Courtesy, The Robert Treat Hotel, Newark, New Jersey

2 parts gin
1 part benedictine
2 dashes curaçao (Cointreau, Triple Sec or Grand Marnier may be substituted)
Ice

Shake. Strain into cocktail glass.

AUNT EMILY

Courtesy, Sloppy Joe's Bar, Havana

¼ orange juice
Drops of grenadine
¼ applejack
¼ gin
¼ apricot brandy

Shake with cracked ice and serve in cocktail glass.

AURUM

Courtesy, Hotel Excelsior, Rome

> 1 part aurum
> 1 part gin
> ½ part orange juice
> ½ part Italian vermouth

Shake in ice with orange peel, and serve in a cocktail glass.

Landlord, fill the flowing bowl
Until it doth run over;
For tonight we'll merry be,
Tomorrow we'll be sober.

Three Jolly Postboys
(18th-century song)

BABY TITTY

A popular preprohibition after-dinner drink.

⅓ anisette liqueur
⅓ crème Yvette
⅓ whipped cream

Use a sherry glass, and pour ingredients carefully on edge of glass, so that the liqueurs do not mix. Top with maraschino cherry.

BACARDI

Juice ½ lime
1 teaspoon grenadine
1 jigger white Bacardi

Shake well with finely chopped ice. Strain and serve in cocktail glass.

BACARDI (frozen)

Juice ½ lime
1 teaspoon grenadine
1 jigger white Bacardi

Pour in electric mixer with shaved ice. Mix and serve, ice and all, in cocktail glass.

BALKAN

Courtesy, The Colony Restaurant, New York City

⅓ vodka
⅓ Pernod
⅓ raki
1 dash Peychaud bitters
Ice

Shake well and serve in cocktail glass.

BALLANTINE MANHATTAN

By Charles Berns, "21" Brands, Inc., New York City

1 part Tribuno sweet vermouth
2 or 3 parts Ballantine Scotch whisky

Stir in mixing glass with ice and 2 slices of orange peel. Strain into cocktail glass.

36 : *Bottoms Up*

BALTIMORE EGGNOG

> 1 fresh egg
> ½ tablespoon sugar
> 1 oz. brandy
> 1 oz. Jamaica rum
> 1 oz. Madeira
> ½ pint fresh milk
>
> *Break egg into shaker. Add ice and ingredients. Shake well and strain into long highball glass. Grate a little nutmeg on top.*

BAMBOO

> ½ jigger sherry
> ½ jigger French vermouth
> 2 dashes of orange bitters
> Ice
>
> *Stir. Strain into cocktail glass.*

BANG

By George Frazier, "Painting the Town with Esquire"

"This is served around ten in the morning at Siasconset on Nantucket."

> 5 parts Plymouth gin
> 1 part dry vermouth
> Few liberal dashes Ojen
>
> *Mix as in a Martini. Add ice and stir. If the proper amount of Ojen is used, the gin flavor should be almost entirely disguised. Serve in cocktail glass.*

BAROQUE

Courtesy, The Baroque Restaurant, New York City

> 1 part fresh lime juice
> ½ teaspoon sugar
> 2 parts Jamaica rum
> 1 part imported gin
> 1 dash imported maraschino
> Ice
>
> *Shake lime juice and sugar well. Add rum and gin. Shake well and serve in iced glass. Float maraschino.*

BAUR AU LAC

Courtesy, Hotel Baur au Lac, Zurich

¼ kirsch
¾ cherry brandy
⅛ lemon juice
⅛ orange juice
Ice

Shake. Serve in cocktail glass.

BEES' KNEES

Courtesy, Hotel Ritz, Paris

Juice ¼ lemon
1 teaspoon honey
½ glass gin

*Dissolve honey in lemon juice, add gin and ice.
Shake well and serve in cocktail glass.*

BEFORE LUNCH

By Joe Pandl, Maitre d'Hotel, Duquesne Club, Pittsburgh

1 lump sugar
2 oz. apple brandy
2 oz. water

*Crush sugar in old-fashioned glass. Add ice and
ingredients. Stir well.*

BEL-AIR

Courtesy, Hotel Bel-Air, Los Angeles

1 jigger Southern Comfort
1 dash dry vermouth
Juice 1 fresh lime

*Mix in electric mixer with shaved ice and serve
in 3-oz. cocktail glass.*

BELLEVUE-PALACE

Courtesy, Hotel Bellevue-Palace, Berne

1 dash Angostura bitters
1/6 Italian vermouth
1/6 Noilly Prat
1/6 Cointreau
1/6 lemon juice
2/6 Scotch whisky
Ice

Shake. Serve in cocktail glass.

BELVEDERE

Courtesy, The Belvedere, Baltimore

1/2 Belvedere rye
1/2 sweet vermouth
1 dash curaçao
Cherry, or lemon peel
Ice

Shake. Serve in cocktail glass. Decorate with cherry or lemon peel.

BENICOT

Courtesy, Embassy Club, The Windsor, Montreal

Juice 1 lime
1/2 oz. apricot brandy
1/2 oz. benedictine

Shake in fine ice and serve with cherry in cocktail glass.

BERKELEY

Courtesy, Berkeley Hotel, London

1/2 gin
1/4 crème de noyau
1/4 lemon juice
1 dash cassis
Ice

Shake well and strain into cocktail glass.

BERMUDA HIGHBALL

¾ jigger brandy
¾ jigger dry gin
½ jigger dry vermouth
1 ice cube

Pour into 6-oz. highball glass. Fill with ginger ale or soda, and stir. Serve with lemon peel.

BERNS MANHATTAN (dry)
By Charles Berns, "21" Brands, Inc., New York City

1 part Tribuno dry vermouth
2 or 3 parts "21" Brands Club Special
    blended whisky

Stir in mixing glass with ice. Strain into cocktail glass. Twist and drop lemon peel into cocktail.

BETWEEN THE SHEETS
Courtesy, Detroit Wonder Bar, Detroit

⅓ Cointreau
⅓ brandy
⅓ benedictine

Add cracked ice and shake well. Serve in cocktail glass.

BEVERLY
Courtesy, Beverly Country Club, New Orleans

1¼ oz. St. James rum
¼ oz. Cuban rum
Dash orange curaçao
¼ oz. pineapple juice
¼ oz. lime juice
½ teaspoon powdered sugar
Ice

Shake. Serve in cocktail glass.

BEVERLY PICKUP
Courtesy, Beverly Country Club, New Orleans

> 1 oz. cognac
> 1 oz. Dubonnet
> 1 oz. dry sherry
> Twist lemon peel
> Ice
>
> *Stir. Serve in cocktail glass.*

BEVERLY WILSHIRE HOTEL
Courtesy, Beverly Wilshire, Beverly Hills

> 1 jigger orange juice
> 1 jigger White Label rum
> 1 dash grenadine
> Ice
>
> *Shake well. Serve in champagne glass garnished with fruit in season.*

BIG LIFT
By Paul Rothmann, Rothmann's East Norwich Inn, East Norwich, Long Island

> 4 oz. chilled champagne
> 1 oz. cognac
> 1 dash Cointreau
> 1 ice cube
>
> *Use 5-oz. champagne glass. Stir gently.*

BIJOU

> 2 dashes Angostura bitters
> ½ jigger French vermouth
> ½ jigger Grand Marnier
> Ice
>
> *Stir. Strain into cocktail glass.*

41 : *Cocktails and Mixed Drinks*

BILLY WILKERSON TOPPER
By Billy Wilkerson, Hollywood, Calif.

Dash orange flower water
1 oz. white Bacardi
½ oz. yellow chartreuse
Pinch of sugar
White of 1 egg
Ice

Mix in electric mixer and serve in a champagne glass.

BIRD & BOTTLE COLLINS
Courtesy, The Bird & Bottle Inn, Garrison, New York

Juice 1 lemon
1 full teaspoon powdered sugar
2 oz. gin
12 to 15 mint leaves removed from stems

Mix above in shaker filled with cubed ice and shake vigorously for about a minute. Strain into 12-oz. glass filled with ice cubes. Top with a dash of soda water and decorate with a sprig of mint.

BIRD & BOTTLE OLD-FASHIONED
Courtesy, The Bird & Bottle Inn, Garrison, New York

2 oz. your favorite whisky
Light dash Angostura bitters
3 dashes orange bitters
½ scant teaspoon powdered sugar
1 thin piece lemon peel
1 thin piece orange peel
1 tablespoon water (never soda water)

Into the bottom of an old-fashioned glass place everything except the whisky. With a wooden muddler press peels to extract oils. Fill glass with cracked (not crushed) ice and pour whisky over it. Stir for about 15 seconds until well chilled. (Rum, applejack or brandy may also be substituted.)

BLACK ROSE

2 dashes grenadine
2 dashes Peychaud bitters
1 jigger Schenley Reserve whisky

Stir, and serve in a champagne glass with cracked ice and twist lemon peel.

BLACK VELVET

½ pint chilled stout or porter
½ pint chilled champagne

Pour both in highball glass.

BLACKBERRY JULEP

2 oz. blackberry brandy
4 sprigs fresh mint
1 lump sugar

Fill tall glass with crushed ice and set it aside. In old-fashioned glass crush sugar with a stick. Add mint leaves and bruise slightly. Add blackberry brandy and mix all together. Pour over the crushed ice in tall glass. Stir until outside of glass is frosted. Decorate with large sprig of mint on top and sprinkle with powdered sugar.

BLOCKBUSTER

By Hal Block, Radio and TV Comedy Star

1 jigger Coronet brandy
½ jigger Schenley Reserve
½ jigger curaçao
Ice

Shake well, strain over cracked ice into old-fashioned glass. Decorate with twist orange peel.

BLOODLESS MARY (nonalcoholic)
By Roscoe F. Oakes, San Francisco

4 oz. tomato juice
Juice ½ lemon
1 teaspoon Worcestershire sauce
½ teaspoon sugar
Salt and pepper to taste
1 dash celery salt
Ice

Shake vigorously. Strain into old-fashioned glass over one cube of ice. Decorate with sprig of fresh mint.

BLOODY BLOODY MARY
By Ted Saucier

1½ oz. vodka
3 oz. tomato juice
½ teaspoon Worcestershire sauce
Juice ½ lemon
Salt, pepper
¼ teaspoon sugar
Dash celery salt
Cracked ice

Shake vigorously and serve in old-fashioned glass over a lump of ice. Decorate with sprig of fresh mint.

BLOODY MARY
Courtesy, Hotel Del Monte, Del Monte, California

½ vodka
½ tomato juice
Dash lemon juice

Serve in old-fashioned glass with a chunk of ice.

BLOODY MARY A LA MILO

By Milo J. Sutliff, Publisher, New York City

2 oz. tomato juice
1 oz. clam juice
1 teaspoon Worcestershire sauce
2 oz. vodka
Cracked ice

Stir tomato juice and clam juice together, and add Worcestershire. Pour this mixture over one inch of cracked ice in a blender or mixer. Add vodka. Turn switch and agitate for 10 seconds. Serve in 3-oz. glass. (This makes 2 cocktails.)

BLUE FLORIDA PAM PAM

By Paul Girault, Bartender, Café de la Paix, Paris

½ gin
½ vodka
Few drops maraschino
1 drop blue vegetable coloring
Ice

Shake well and strain into cocktail glass.

BLUE GRASS

Courtesy, Gene Leone, of Leone Restaurant fame

This is one of the most palatable drinks originated, appropriate both as a cocktail and as an after-dinner drink.

Juice ½ small lemon
1 oz. golden rum
⅓ oz. green crème de menthe
3 leaves fresh mint
Shaved ice

Blend in electric mixer. Add 3 dashes banana cordial. Pour into champagne glass. Decorate with sprig of fresh mint, which has been dipped in powdered sugar.

BLUE MONDAY

¾ jigger vodka
¼ jigger Cointreau
1 dash blue curaçao
Ice

Shake well. Strain into cocktail glass.

BLUEBEARD'S PLANTERS PUNCH
Courtesy, Bluebeard's Castle Hotel, Saint Thomas, Virgin Islands

1 barspoon sugar
1 jigger heavy rum (Myers or Carioca)
Juice ½ lime
1 dash Angostura bitters
Cracked ice

Shake and serve in highball glass. Add cherry and nutmeg.

BOCANA SPECIAL
Courtesy, Hotel de Las Americas, Acapulco

⅕ grapefruit juice
⅕ Gordon gin
⅕ Parfait Amour
⅕ vermouth Cinzano
⅕ Spanish manzanilla
Few drops Angostura bitters

Shake in cocktail shaker with cracked ice. Sugar the edge of a champagne glass and serve, decorated with cherries and orange sections. Float a mint leaf on top.

BOURBON COBBLER

3 oz. bourbon
1 teaspoon sugar

Fill wine goblet ¼ full with cracked ice, add bourbon and sugar. Fill glass with water. Stir well. Decorate with half a slice of orange, a maraschino cherry, and a pineapple stick.

Bottoms Up

By AL DORNE

1 jigger Coronet brandy
½ jigger curaçao
1 barspoon grenadine
1 barspoon heavy cream
Yolk 1 egg
Ice

Shake well. Strain into cocktail glass.

BOURBON DAISY

Juice ½ lemon
½ teaspoon powdered sugar
6 dashes grenadine
1 jigger bourbon

Half fill a highball glass with finely cracked ice. Stir until glass is frosted. Pour ingredients over ice. Fill with soda water. Decorate with a sprig of fresh mint, a slice of lemon, and a slice of orange.

BOURBON EGGNOG

1 jigger bourbon
1 egg
1 teaspoon sugar
½ pint milk

Put into shaker with ice and shake well. Strain into 12-oz. goblet. Top with grated nutmeg.

BOURBON HIGHBALL

1 jigger bourbon
Cracked ice
Club soda or ginger ale

A tall drink, served in a large highball glass. Pour liquor over ice and add soda or ginger ale.

BOURBON OLD-FASHIONED

1 cube sugar
Dash Angostura bitters
1½ oz. bourbon

Muddle sugar and bitters in old-fashioned glass with a dash of soda water. Add cracked ice, bourbon. Stir. Decorate with half a slice of orange, a maraschino cherry and a stick of fresh pineapple.

BOURBON ON THE ROCKS

1 jigger of bourbon
Dash of water (plain or soda)
Twist of lemon peel (if desired)

Fill an old-fashioned glass with cracked ice. Pour in bourbon, add water and lemon peel.

BOURBON RICKEY

Juice and rind of ½ lime
Lump of ice
1 jigger bourbon

Fill with soda water. Serve in Delmonico glass.

BOURBON SLING

1 lump sugar
1 teaspoon water
1 jigger bourbon
1 piece twisted lemon peel
1 lump ice

Dissolve sugar in water in an old-fashioned glass. Add bourbon, lemon peel and ice. Stir. Add grated nutmeg, and serve with small spoon.

BOURBON SMASH

3 sprigs fresh mint
2 teaspoons water
½ teaspoon sugar
1 jigger bourbon
Cracked ice

Muddle mint, sugar and water carefully in an old-fashioned glass. Add bourbon and ice. Serve with small spoon.

BOURBON SOUR

Juice of ½ lemon
½ teaspoon sugar
1 jigger bourbon
Ice

Shake well. Strain into Delmonico glass. Dash of siphon. Decorate with half an orange slice and cherry.

BOURBON TODDY

1 lump sugar
3 teaspoons water
1 jigger bourbon
1 lump ice
Dash nutmeg

Dissolve sugar in water in old-fashioned glass. Add liquor, ice and nutmeg. Serve with teaspoon. For a Hot Bourbon Toddy, leave out the ice and add hot water. Serve with teaspoon.

BRANDINI

By Jimmy Starr, Motion Picture Editor, Los Angeles Herald *and Express*

2 parts old brandy
1 part dry vermouth
Ice

Stir and chill in typical Martini fashion. Serve with an olive, in cocktail glass.

BRANDY AND SODA

1 jigger brandy
Cracked ice

Fill highball glass with soda water.

BRANDY COBBLER

3 oz. brandy
1 teaspoonful sugar

Fill wine goblet ¼ full with cracked ice. Add sugar and brandy. Fill glass with water. Stir well. Decorate with half slice of orange, a maraschino cherry, and a pineapple stick.

BRANDY COLLINS

Juice ½ lemon
½ teaspoon powdered sugar
1 jigger brandy

Shake well and strain into Collins glass. Add lump of ice and fill glass with soda water.

49 : *Cocktails and Mixed Drinks*

BRANDY DAISY

Juice ½ lemon
½ teaspoon powdered sugar
6 dashes grenadine
1 jigger brandy

Half fill a highball glass with finely cracked ice. Stir until glass is frosted. Pour ingredients over ice. Fill with soda water. Decorate with a sprig of fresh mint, a slice of orange, and a slice of lemon.

BRANDY EGGNOG

1 jigger brandy
1 egg
1 teaspoon sugar
½ pint milk

Put into shaker with ice and shake well. Strain into 12-oz. goblet. Top with grated nutmeg.

BRANDY FIX

1 teaspoon sugar
1 teaspoon water
Juice ½ lemon
½ jigger cherry brandy
1 jigger brandy

Dissolve sugar in water in old-fashioned glass. Add remainder of ingredients. Fill glass with fine ice. Stir gently. Add slice of lemon and serve with straw.

BRANDY FLIP

1 jigger brandy
½ teaspoon of sugar
1 whole egg
Ice

Shake, strain. Pour into fizz glass. Grate nutmeg on top.

BRANDY HIGHBALL

1 jigger brandy
Cracked ice

Fill highball glass with charged water.

BRANDY ON THE ROCKS
1 jigger brandy

Fill old-fashioned glass with cracked ice. Pour in brandy. Add dash of water, or charged water. Also twist of lemon peel, if desired.

BRANDY PUNCH
Juice ½ lemon
1 teaspoon sugar
1 jigger brandy

Place ingredients in a tall highball glass. Fill with shaved ice. Add soda water. Decorate with orange slice, maraschino cherry, pineapple stick. Serve with straws.

BRANDY SANGAREE
1½ jiggers brandy
2 dashes Angostura bitters
¼ teaspoon sugar
1 jigger water
Ice

Stir. Serve in fizz glass.

BRANDY SLING
1 lump sugar
1 teaspoon water
1 jigger brandy
1 piece twisted lemon peel
1 lump ice

Dissolve sugar in water in old-fashioned glass. Stir. Add grated nutmeg. Serve with small spoon.

BRANDY SMASH
½ teaspoon sugar
2 teaspoons water
1 jigger brandy
3 sprigs fresh mint

Place mint, sugar and water in old-fashioned glass. Muddle carefully. Add brandy and cracked ice. Serve with small spoon.

51 : *Cocktails and Mixed Drinks*

BRANDY SOUR

Juice ½ lemon
½ barspoon powdered sugar
1 jigger brandy
Ice

Shake well and strain into Delmonico glass. Add dash of club soda, half a slice of orange, and a cherry.

BRANDY TODDY

1 lump sugar
3 teaspoonsful water
1 jigger brandy
Lump of ice
Dash of nutmeg

Dissolve sugar in water in old-fashioned glass. Add brandy, ice, and nutmeg. Serve with teaspoon. For Hot Brandy Toddy, leave out ice, add hot water. Serve with teaspoon.

BROADWAY AND ELSEWHERE
In Honor of Jack Lait, Columnist, New York Mirror

Juice ¼ lemon
½ jigger green chartreuse
1 jigger Schenley gin
Ice

Shake well, and strain into chilled cocktail glass. Decorate with maraschino cherry.

BROADWAY BUGLE
By Dan Parker, Sports Columnist, New York Mirror and International News Service

Juice ½ lime
Juice ¼ lemon
1 jigger white Bacardi
1 dash maraschino cordial
1 barspoon sugar

Shake well with cracked ice and serve in cocktail glass.

BROADWAY THIRST
By Harry Craddock, American Bar, The Dorchester, London

½ tequila
¼ orange juice
¼ lemon juice
1 teaspoon sirup
Ice

Shake, strain, and serve in cocktail glass.

BRONCO BUSTER
Courtesy, Arizona Biltmore, Phoenix

1 jigger applejack
1 jigger Schenley Reserve whisky
½ jigger curaçao
Juice ½ lemon
Ice

Shake well. Serve over cracked ice in old-fashioned glass. Decorate with twist of orange peel.

BRONX

⅔ jigger gin
⅓ jigger orange juice
1 dash French vermouth
1 dash Italian vermouth
Ice

Shake. Strain into cocktail glass.

BROUSSARD
Courtesy, Broussard Restaurant, New Orleans

3 dashes simple sirup
1 dash Peychaud bitters
1 oz. good bourbon whisky
Small twist lemon peel
2 dashes absinthe

Serve in old-fashioned glass filled with ice chopped not too fine and top with absinthe.

53 : *Cocktails and Mixed Drinks*

BROWN PALACE HOTEL

Courtesy, The Brown Palace Hotel, Denver

2 dashes orange bitters
2 dashes maraschino
2 dashes Herbsaint
⅓ French vermouth
⅔ London dry gin
Ice

Shake well and strain into cocktail glass with an olive.

BUDGET BLUES

By Cedric Gibbons, Hollywood's Leading Scenic Designer

1 dash grenadine
1 dash raspberry sirup
Juice ½ lemon
1 jigger white rum
½ jigger curaçao
Shaved ice

Blend in electric mixer. Serve in champagne glass with small sprig of fresh mint.

BULLFROG

Courtesy, Embassy Club, The Windsor, Montreal

Juice ½ lime
1¼ oz. Canadian rye
¾ oz. apricot brandy

Shake with fine ice and serve with cherry in cocktail glass.

BULLFROG

By Donald B. Tansil, New York City

1 oz. DuBouchett green crème de menthe
1 oz. Otard brandy
1 oz. crème de cacao
1 oz. heavy cream
Ice

Shake well and strain into saucer champagne glass.

Brownie

By ARTHUR WILLIAM BROWN

1 oz. Coronet brandy
1 oz. crème de cacao
1 oz. heavy cream
1 dash kirschwasser
Ice

Shake well, and strain into cocktail glass. Decorate with maraschino cherry.

BUTTERY COOLER
Courtesy, Ambassador West, Chicago

> 2 jiggers golden rum
> 1 jigger lemon juice
> 1 teaspoon sugar

Shake and pour over shaved ice in Collins glass. Float Burgundy wine on top and decorate with maraschino cherry.

BY THE SEA
By Ed Taws, Bucks County, Pennsylvania

This recipe is a big improvement over the original Stinger, which consists of ⅓ white crème de menthe and ⅔ brandy. The green crème de menthe gives the cocktail the cool, green appearance of the ocean, and the brandy and kirschwasser its potency.

> ⅓ green crème de menthe
> ⅔ brandy
> Dash kirschwasser
> Ice

Mix in electric mixer, and serve frappéed in cocktail glass.

Let us have wine and women, mirth and laughter,
Sermons and soda water the day after.
             GEORGE GORDON, LORD BYRON
             (Don Juan)

CALIFORNIA WINE CUP
By Ted Saucier

This is a delightful summer drink to serve during dinner or to order when you are whiling away an evening at your favorite night club.

1 bottle California sauterne
2 oz. California brandy
2 oz. Cointreau or Grand Marnier
3 teaspoons powdered sugar
1 pint charged water

Place several large pieces of cracked ice in a large glass pitcher. Pour ingredients over ice. Decorate with a few slices of lemon and orange, and other fruit in season, such as fresh strawberries cut in two, or sliced fresh peaches. Also add sprig of fresh mint over which a teaspoonful of powdered sugar has been sprayed. Muddle lightly with long barspoon and serve in wine goblets.

CALIFORNIA ZEPHYR

Recalling the gentle California breezes and several delightful trips on the luxurious train bearing that same name.

½ jigger applejack
½ jigger Coronet brandy
1 barspoon apricot brandy
1 dash absinthe
Ice

Shake well. Strain into cocktail glass, and drop in twist orange peel.

CALIFORNIE PALACE
Courtesy, Californie Palace, Cannes

⅓ gin
⅔ French vermouth
⅓ maraschino
⅙ green chartreuse
Ice

Shake well and strain into cocktail glass. Add small chunk of pineapple.

CANADIAN

By J. H. Campbell, Canadian Pacific Railway, Montreal

2 parts bonded rye
1 part pure Canadian maple sirup
Ice

Chill and stir. Strain into cocktail glass.

CARIOCA

Juice ½ lime
1½ oz. Carioca rum
1 barspoon sugar
Dash maraschino liqueur

Shake with finely shaved ice and serve in cocktail glass.

CARIOCA COLLINS

Juice ½ lemon
½ barspoon powdered sugar
1 jigger Carioca rum

Shake well and strain into Collins glass. Add lump of ice and fill glass with soda water.

CARIOCA EGGNOG

1 egg
1 tablespoon powdered sugar
1 jigger (1½ oz.) Carioca rum
1 glass milk

Break egg into shaker. Add ice and ingredients. Shake well and strain into tall highball glass. Grate a little nutmeg on top.

CARLTON HOTEL SPECIAL

Courtesy, Carlton Hotel, Cannes

Juice ½ lemon
⅔ cognac
⅓ white curaçao
1 teaspoon barley sirup
Ice

Shake. Strain into cocktail glass.

59 : *Cocktails and Mixed Drinks*

CARLYLE PICK-ME-UP

Courtesy, The Carlyle Hotel, New York City

⅔ bourbon
⅓ lemon juice
1 dash Pernod absinthe
Ice

Shake. Strain into cocktail glass.

CARNAVAL ROOM

Courtesy, The Sherry-Netherland, New York City

3 parts vodka
3 dashes French vermouth

Rinse the glass out with some tangerine liqueur and discard the liqueur. Ice. Stir and strain into a chilled cocktail glass. Drop in a large black olive.

CARRERA HOTEL

Courtesy, Hotel Carrera, Santiago

2 soupspoons canned strawberries
3 soupspoons rum
1 soupspoon orange juice
1 soupspoon Cointreau
1 soupspoon vermouth Cinzano
2 drops Angostura bitters
Sugar
Ice

Shake and strain into old-fashioned glass.

CARRERE

Courtesy, Maurice Carrere, Owner of the Famous Auberge de la Moutière, Montfort l'Amaury, France

3 leaves fresh mint
½ lump sugar
Dash crème de cacao
Lump ice
Dry French champagne

Place mint in a large saucer champagne glass. Add sugar, crème de cacao and ice. Fill glass with well-chilled champagne.

CATHERINE ALEXANDRIA
Courtesy, Olmsted's, Washington, D. C.

Initiated by Leonard Mitchell for Miss Catherine of Alexandria

⅔ crème de cacao
⅓ gin

Stir well with ice and pour into sherry glass. Top with a floater of cream. When you start sipping on this, it will look like a geyser.

CAVALIER
Courtesy, The Cavalier Hotel, Virginia Beach

½ oz. benedictine
1 oz. brandy
4 oz. champagne
Juice 1 lime
Ice

Shake and strain into champagne glass.

CHALET COCHAND
Courtesy, Chalet Cochand, Laurentian Mountains, Quebec

½ jigger rum
½ jigger sherry
4 dashes lemon juice
Ice

Shake. Strain into cocktail glass.

CHAMPAGNE COCKTAIL
Champagne
Lump of sugar
Dash Angostura bitters
Lump of ice

Place sugar in champagne glass. Add bitters and ice. Fill glass with chilled champagne. Top with twist of lemon peel.

61 : *Cocktails and Mixed Drinks*

CHAMPAGNE PUNCH (serve in bowl)

    1 quart champagne
    1 quart sauterne
    1 pint soda water
    6 teaspoons powdered sugar
    1 sliced orange
    1 sliced lemon

Scoop out center of large ice block. Then place in bowl and decorate with maraschino cherries and sprigs of fresh mint.

CHAMPAGNE ROOM
Courtesy, El Morocco, New York

    Champagne
    1 ice cube
    Dash Cointreau
    Dash brandy

Place ice in champagne glass. Pour Cointreau and brandy over it. Fill with imported champagne. Add twist of lemon peel.

CHANTECLAIR
Courtesy, The Sherry-Netherland, New York City

    3 parts gin
    1 part sherry (dry)
    2 drops absinthe or absinthe substitute
    Ice

Stir well and pour into chilled glass. Put a lemon peel on top.

CHANTECLER SPECIAL
Courtesy, The Chantecler, Ste. Adele en Haut, Quebec

    1 part Calvados
    1 part apricot brandy
    1 part gin
    1 part orange juice
    Ice

Shake. Strain into cocktail glass.

CHAPLIN'S SPECIAL GIBSON

By W. W. "Bill" Chaplin, National Broadcasting Company,
New York City

> 1 part gin
> ½ teaspoon juice from onion bottle
>
> *Stir well with cracked ice in shaker and pour over*
> *a pearl onion into a chilled glass.*

CHARLES COBURN

By Charles Coburn, Motion Picture Star

> ½ gin
> ½ canned pineapple juice
> Juice ½ lemon
>
> *Mix with ice and shake well. Strain into cocktail*
> *glass. Garnish with small piece lemon peel.*

CHASEN'S

By John Dionne, Head Bartender, Chasen's, Los Angeles
John Dionne's prize-winning concoction in a competition with hundreds of other leading bartenders, as the most original, pleasing, and smoothest. ". . . only two to a customer!"

> Pink champagne
> 1½ oz. Southern Comfort
> ¾ oz. red Passionola or wild cherry sirup
> Juice 1 small lime
>
> *Shake well with ice and serve, ice and all, in*
> *unusual squat glass. Then serve 4-oz. bottle*
> *Renault pink champagne in individual bucket,*
> *well iced, to fill glass. This is topped by a dash*
> *of fresh mint.*

CHATEAU FRONTENAC SPECIAL

Courtesy, Chateau Frontenac, Quebec

"This cocktail was featured particularly during the two World Conferences which were held at this hotel, and went over in a big way with our guests, who came from practically all over the world."

¼ orange juice
¼ Gordon's dry gin
¼ Grand Marnier
¼ brandy
Ice

Shake and strain into cocktail glass.

CHATHAM HOTEL FLYER

Courtesy, The Chatham, New York City

1½ oz. white rum
½ teaspoon sugar
Mint leaves
Lemon juice
Ice

Shake well, strain into champagne glass and top with champagne.

CHATHAM HOTEL SPECIAL

Courtesy, The Chatham, New York City

1 dash crème de cacao
½ oz. cream
1½ oz. brandy
½ oz. port wine
Ice

Shake well and serve in cocktail glass.

CHIEF SPECIAL

Courtesy, Atchison, Topeka and Santa Fe Railway

1 jigger lemon juice
1 jigger orange juice
1 jigger green crème de menthe

Place lemon and orange juice in mixing glass with shaved ice. Add crème de menthe. Shake well and serve in Delmonico glass. Garnish with maraschino cheery.

CHINA

Courtesy, Hotel Excelsior, Rome

1 part China Martini
2 parts Campari bitters
1 slice orange

Shake well in ice. Strain into cocktail glass.

CHOLLY KNICKERBOCKER

In Honor of Igor Cassini, Author of the "Cholly Knickerbocker" Column, International News Service

Ice cube
2 dashes raspberry cordial
Champagne

Put ice and cordial in a saucer champagne glass. Fill glass with champagne and decorate with thin slice of lemon.

CHRISTY FOX

By Christy Fox, Society Columnist, Los Angeles Times

1 teaspoon pineapple juice
1 teaspoon lemon or lime juice
1 teaspoon grenadine
1 jigger gin

Shake well with cracked ice and serve in a chilled cocktail glass.

CHRISTY GIRL

Courtesy, Howard Chandler Christy Room, The Sherry-Netherland, New York City

½ jigger DuBouchett peach brandy
½ jigger dry gin
Dash grenadine
White 1 egg
Ice

Shake well and strain into cocktail glass. Decorate with maraschino cherry.

CIRO'S SPECIAL

Courtesy, Ciro's, Hollywood

Juice 1 fresh lime
1 jigger dark rum
½ jigger crème de cassis
1 dash Grand Marnier
Ice

Shake and strain into cocktail glass.

CITY HOTEL NO. 1

Courtesy, City Hotel, Buenos Aires

2 dashes yellow chartreuse
½ Hesperidina Bagley
½ Quinado Trapiche
Ice

Serve in old-fashioned glass with slice of orange on top. Cool in glass before serving.

CITY HOTEL NO. 2

Courtesy, City Hotel, Buenos Aires

2 dashes yellow chartreuse
½ vermouth Americano Gancia
½ Dubonnet
Ice

Serve in old-fashioned glass with slice of orange on top. Cool in glass before serving.

CLAREMONT

Courtesy, Hotel Claremont, Berkeley

1 dash orange curaçao
1 oz. soda water
1 oz. good bourbon
Lemon peel
Angostura bitters
Ice

Serve in old-fashioned glass. (The curaçao is used instead of sugar.)

CLARET AND SAUTERNE PUNCH (serve in bowl)

2 jiggers brandy
2 jiggers curacao
3 tablespoons powdered sugar
Juice 3 lemons
1 quart claret
1 quart sauterne
1 quart soda water

*Place large ice block in center of bowl and mix.
Scoop out center of ice block and decorate with
maraschino cherries and sprigs of fresh mint.*

CLARET COBBLER

1 teaspoon sugar
3 oz. claret

*Fill wine goblet ¼ full with cracked ice. Add
sugar and claret. Fill glass with water and stir
well. Decorate with half an orange slice, maraschino cherry and pineapple stick.*

CLARET CUP WALDORF (as served at the old Waldorf-Astoria)

½ teaspoon sugar
1½ ponies brandy
1 pony benedictine
1 pony maraschino

*Put into mixing glass and fill with seltzer. Stir
and pour into pitcher. Add large block of ice, a
bottle of claret, and fruit. Decorate with frosted
mint.*

CLARET LEMONADE

Juice 1 lemon
1 teaspoon powdered sugar
1 lump ice
1 jigger (1-1½ oz.) claret

*Squeeze lemon into an 8- or 10-oz. lemonade or
highball glass. Add other ingredients and fill glass
with club soda. Decorate with a half slice of
lemon and maraschino cherry.*

67 : *Cocktails and Mixed Drinks*

CLARET ORANGEADE

Juice 1 orange
1 teaspoon powdered sugar
1 lump ice
1 jigger (1-1½ oz.) claret

Squeeze orange into an 8- or 10-oz. lemonade or highball glass. Add other ingredients and fill glass with club soda. Decorate with a half slice of orange and maraschino cherry.

CLARET PUNCH

Juice ½ lemon
1 teaspoon sugar
1½ jiggers claret
Ice

Add small quantity of water to fill. Stir. Pour into goblet. Decorate with fresh fruit.

CLARIDGE
Courtesy, Claridge's, London

⅓ dry gin
⅓ French vermouth
⅙ apricot brandy
⅙ Cointreau
Ice

Shake well and strain into cocktail glass.

CLARIDGE PUNCHINELLO
Courtesy, Mayfair Lounge, The Claridge Hotel, Atlantic City

19 oz. brandy
9 oz. dark rum
2 oz. 151-proof rum
1 oz. kirschwasser
1 oz. Dubonnet

Serve by putting 3 oz. of the punch into a large punch glass. Fill glass with cracked ice and garnish with cherries and half a slice of orange (These ingredients for one quart Claridge Punchinello.)

CLOAK AND DAGGER

Courtesy, Hotel Astor, New York City

> 1 part gold rum
> ½ part Dagger rum
> 1 teaspoon sugar
> 1 part lime juice
>
> *Mix with fine ice in electric mixer and serve in a champagne glass.*

CLOISTER

Courtesy, The Cloister, Sea Island, Georgia

> 1¼ oz. gin
> ¼ oz. apricot brandy
> ¼ oz. grenadine
> Ice
>
> *Shake well and serve in cocktail glass.*

CLOVER CLUB

> Juice ½ lemon
> ½ teaspoon sugar
> ½ pony raspberry sirup
> ½ pony white of egg
> 1 jigger gin
> Ice
>
> *Shake well. Strain into cocktail glass.*

COBBLER

A summer drink made of iced wine or spirits and sugar, served in a wine goblet and decorated with fresh fruit after the ingredients are mixed.

> 1 teaspoon sugar
> 1½ jiggers wine or spirits
>
> *Add a little water and ice. Mix and decorate with fruit in season—either a fresh strawberry, slice of lemon or a slice of orange and a maraschino cherry. Serve in wine goblet. A cobbler may be made with applejack, claret or other wines, bourbon, brandy, Dubonnet, gin, rum, rye, sherry, Southern Comfort, sloe gin, port, vermouth or vodka.*

COBINA WRIGHT

By Cobina Wright, Society Columnist, Los Angeles Herald
and Express

Cliquot ginger ale
4 tablespoons lemon juice (freshly squeezed)
1 tablespoon honey
1 large wine glass applejack (more, if needed)

*Fill electric mixer half full of ginger ale. Add
cracked ice and other ingredients and mix. Serve
in highball glass.*

COCK 'N BULL SPECIAL

Courtesy, The Cock 'n Bull, Hollywood

½ oz. brandy
¾ oz. benedictine
¾ oz. bourbon
¼ oz. Cointreau
Ice

*Stir. Pour over cube of ice in large chilled cham-
pagne glass. Garnish with twist of orange peel.*

COCK O' THE ROOST

By Adolphe Menjou, Motion Picture and TV Star

½ jigger orange juice
½ jigger French vermouth
½ jigger Italian vermouth
½ jigger white rum
½ jigger benedictine
Ice

*Shake well. Strain into cocktail glass. Decorate
with half a slice of orange.*

COCKTAIL DE LA LOUISIANE
Courtesy, La Louisiane, New Orleans

⅓ jigger rye whisky
⅓ jigger Italian vermouth
⅓ jigger benedictine
3 dashes absinthe substitute
3 dashes Peychaud bitters

Mix in bar glass with cracked ice. Strain into cocktail glass in which has been placed a maraschino cherry.

COCOANUT FROST
Courtesy, The Colony Restaurant, New York City

1 jigger white Cuban rum
2 teaspoons cocoanut frost powder
1 scoop shaved ice

Mix in mixer 3 minutes and serve in champagne glass.

COCOANUT GROVE
Courtesy, The Cocoanut Grove, Los Angeles Ambassador

1½ jiggers light rum
Juice 1 lime
1 teaspoon Cocoanut Mix
2 dashes curaçao
Shaved ice

Mix in electric mixer. Serve in champagne glass.

COCOANUT SNOW
By Louella O. Parsons, Hollywood Columnist

"It is just as good as an ice-cream soda, only more kick."

1 jigger white rum
2 heaping tablespoons Cocoanut Snow
1 egg white
Shaved ice

Put ice and ingredients in mixer. Serve in champagne glass.

COFFEE COCKTAIL

2 oz. port wine
1 oz. brandy
Yolk 1 egg
½ teaspoon sugar
Ice

Shake well. Strain into claret glass.

COFFEE SUPERBA (after-dinner coffee)
By Ted Saucier
After you have dined well there is nothing more delightful.

1 large cup black coffee, very hot
1 pony fine cognac
1 lump sugar
Twist lemon peel
Twist orange peel

*Pour coffee over sugar and add cognac. Drop
lemon and orange peel into coffee after twisting.*

COLLINS

*Tom and John Collinses both are preprohibition
drinks. The Tom Collins is made of Old Tom gin
and the John Collins of Holland gin. Since prohibition and repeal, however, several additions
have been made to the Collins family, including
those made of applejack, bourbon, brandy, rum,
and rye.*

The Collins should be served in a 14-oz. glass.

COLOMBE
By Paul Girault, Bartender, Café de la Paix, Paris

French champagne
Few drops Cherry Rocher
Few drops cognac
Few drops Cointreau
1 slice orange

*Serve with cracked ice. Fill glass with French
champagne.*

COLONY

Courtesy, The Colony Restaurant, New York City

Juice ½ lime
½ Southern Comfort
½ vodka
Ice

Shake and serve in cocktail glass.

COLUMBIA CLUB ENGINEERS' SPECIAL

By Michael Dunn, Head Bartender, Columbia University Club
New York City

1½ oz. Jamaica rum
1 oz. Martinique rum
Juice 1 lime
1 teaspoon sugar

Shake well in mixing glass with cracked ice.
Strain into 12-oz. glass containing an ice cube.
Fill glass with charged water, stir slightly and
serve.

COME UP AND SEE ME SOMETIME

Juice ½ lime
Juice ½ orange
2 oz. white Cuban rum
2 oz. cognac
1 oz. Cointreau
1 oz. grenadine
2 dashes orange water
Ice

Shake vigorously. Serve in 14-oz. Tom Collins
glass, ⅓ full of shaved ice. Decorate with a slice
of fresh lime. Serve with 2 straws.

73 : *Cocktails and Mixed Drinks*

COOL HAND ON THE FEVERED BROW
  By Lowell Thomas, Writer, Lecturer, and Radio Columnist

  1 part fresh lemon juice
  1 part fresh lime juice
  2 parts white Bacardi
  1 part apricot brandy

  Shake with cracked ice and serve in a sugared glass.

COOL O' THE EVENING
  Courtesy, Esquire Magazine

  1 jigger Brugal rum (White Label)
  Juice ¼ lemon
  ½ teaspoon sugar
  Sprig of mint or few drops crème de menthe

  Crush mint, if used. Add ingredients and shake well with ice until frosted. Strain into cocktail glass.

COOLER
  A tall, refreshing drink of Boston origin.

  Juice ½ lemon
  ¼ teaspoon sugar
  1 jigger spirits
  Soda water
  Ice

  A Cooler may be made with claret, Dubonnet, port, sherry, vermouth, or other wines; or with applejack, bourbon, brandy, gin, rum, rye, sloe gin, Southern Comfort, or vodka.

COPACABANA PALACE
  Courtesy, Copacabana Palace Hotel, Rio de Janeiro

  ½ Cinzano
  ½ port wine
  Few drops yellow chartreuse
  Ice

  Shake. Strain into cocktail glass.

COPAIN SPECIAL

Courtesy, Copain Restaurant, New York City

¼ Campari
¾ rye
Ice

Stir. Strain into cocktail glass. Add twist lemon peel over the top.

COPLEY PLAZA

Courtesy, The Copley Plaza, Boston

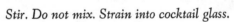

1 part Cointreau
2 parts brandy
1 part Dubonnet
Ice

Stir. Do not mix. Strain into cocktail glass.

CORNELL

½ jigger French vermouth
½ jigger Gordon gin
Ice

Stir. Strain into cocktail glass.

CORNELL SPECIAL

½ jigger dry gin
½ jigger benedictine
Juice ½ lemon
Ice

Stir. Serve in cocktail glass with dash of soda water.

CORONET EGGNOG

1 egg
1 tablespoon powdered sugar
1 jigger (1½ oz.) Coronet brandy
1 glass milk
1 oz. heavy cream

Break egg into shaker. Add ice and ingredients. Shake well and strain into long highball glass. Grate a little nutmeg on top.

75 : *Cocktails and Mixed Drinks*

CRÈME DE MENTHE HIGHBALL

1 ice cube
1⅓ jiggers crème de menthe

Put into 6-oz. highball glass. Fill with soda water and stir slightly.

CREOLE

Courtesy, The Roosevelt, New Orleans

½ French vermouth
½ Italian vermouth
1 dash Herbsaint

Shake well with ice and strain into cocktail glass.

"CRESTA CLUB" ST. MORITZ

By Fred Ammann, Palace Hotel, St. Moritz, Switzerland

½ Booth's gin
⅓ grapefruit juice
⅕ Grand Marnier
Ice

Shake well. Serve in glass with sugar coating on rim.

CRUM BUM

By Toots Shor, Toots Shor Restaurant, New York City

2 jiggers rye whisky
½ jigger Triple Sec
Dash Peychaud bitters

Place cracked ice in a 6-oz. old-fashioned glass. Pour liquor over it, add bitters. Stir. Decorate with thin slice lemon.

CRYSTAL
Courtesy, Beverly Hills Hotel, Beverly Hills

> ½ oz. pineapple juice
> ½ lime
> ½ oz. light rum
> ½ oz. vodka
> 1 dash sugar
> Ice
>
> *Mix in mixer and serve in champagne glass.*

CUB ROOM SPECIAL
Courtesy, The Stork Club, New York City

> ½ peach brandy
> ¼ apricot brandy
> ¼ curaçao
> Juice 1 lime
>
> *Serve in tall glass with shaved ice.*

CUBA LIBRE

> Juice ½ lime
> 3 cubes ice
> 1½ oz. Cuban white rum
> Coca-Cola
>
> *Squeeze juice of lime into 10-oz. Collins glass and drop in lime shell. Add ice rum, and fill glass with Coca-Cola.*

CUBAN RUM COBBLER

> 3 oz. Cuban rum
> 1 teaspoon sugar
>
> *Fill wine goblet ¼ full with cracked ice. Add sugar and rum. Stir well. Decorate with half a slice of orange, a maraschino cherry, and a pineapple stick.*

77 : *Cocktails and Mixed Drinks*

CUBAN RUM SOUR

> Juice ½ lemon
> ½ barspoon powdered sugar
> 1 jigger Cuban rum
> Ice
>
> *Shake well and strain into glass. Add a dash
> of club soda, half a slice of orange, and a cherry.*

CUGAT TRIPLE C—CCC'S
By Xavier Cugat, "The Rhumba King"

> ¾ white rum
> ¼ grenadine
> Dash Pernod (absinthe)
> Juice of ½ lime
> Ice
>
> *Shake well and serve in cocktail glass.*

CUP

A beverage made of wine, usually iced, and with flavoring herbs and fruits,
served in garnished pitchers, to be poured at table.

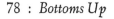

> 1½ ponies of brandy
> 1 pony Cointreau
> 1 pony maraschino
> 1 quart bottle wine
> 1 large piece ice
>
> *Pour ingredients into large glass pitcher. Decorate
> with slices of orange, lemon, maraschino cherry,
> fresh pineapple sticks or slices, strawberries (when
> in season), and sprig of fresh mint. Top the cup
> with half a bottle of soda water.*

CUP: FRUIT CUP (a popular nonalcoholic summer drink)

> 2 oz. raspberry sirup
> 2 oz. strawberry sirup
> 2 oz. pineapple sirup
> or
> 6 oz. grenadine sirup
> Juice 1 lemon
> Juice 1 orange
> Cracked ice

Use one of sirups listed. Add lemon and orange juice, ice. Fill remainder of pitcher with soda water. Decorate with maraschino cherry, orange slice, lemon slice and sprig of fresh mint.

CYPRESS POINT

Courtesy, Del Monte Properties Company, Pebble Beach, California

> ½ Guinness stout
> ½ champagne

Pour very slowly into champagne glass.

CYVA

By Franklin C. Edson, Prominent Yachtsman

> ½ jigger gin
> ½ jigger dry sherry
> 1 teaspoon cognac
> 2 dashes orange bitters
> Ice

Stir. Strain into cocktail glass, and serve with pitted green olive.

If all be true that I do think,
There are five reasons we should drink;
Good wine—a friend—or being dry—
Or lest we should be by and by—
Or any other reason why.

JOHN SIRMOND
(*Causæ Bibendi*)

DAILY DOUBLE

By Robert G. Johnson, President, Old Country Trotting Association, Westbury, Long Island

Juice ½ lemon
1 jigger Schenley Reserve whisky
½ jigger Grand Marnier
Dash Peychaud bitters
Shaved ice

Shake well. Serve frappéed in double cocktail glass. Decorate with twist of orange peel.

DAIQUIRI

Courtesy, The Dearborn Inn, Dearborn, Michigan

Juice 1 fresh lime
1 teaspoon powdered sugar
2 oz. white rum

Shake well with cracked ice. Strain into 3-oz. cocktail glass.

DAIQUIRI (frozen)

Juice ½ lime
½ teaspoon sugar
1 jigger white Bacardi rum

Place in electric mixer with shaved ice. Serve in saucer champagne glass, with 2 short straws.

DAIQUIRI (original)

Juice ½ lime
1 teaspoon powdered sugar
1 jigger Cuban rum

Shake well with finely chopped ice. Strain into cocktail glass and serve.

D'ANGLETERRE

Courtesy, Hotel d'Angleterre, Copenhagen

½ cognac
¼ French vermouth
¼ Italian vermouth
1 dash Angostura bitters
Ice

Shake well and strain into cocktail glass. Squeeze orange peel on top.

DEADLINE

By Thyra Samter Winslow, Short Story Writer and Novelist

¼ jigger Cresta Blanca sherry
1 jigger dry gin
Dash orange bitters
Ice

Stir. Strain into chilled cocktail glass. Drop twist orange peel in glass.

DEARBORN INN MANHATTAN

Courtesy, The Dearborn Inn, Dearborn, Michigan

1 dash bitters
1 oz. Italian vermouth
2 oz. Canadian Club

Stir well with cracked ice. Strain into 3-oz. cocktail glass. Serve with maraschino cherry.

DEL CORONADO
Courtesy, Luau Room, Hotel del Coronado, Coronado, California

½ oz. pineapple juice
Juice ½ orange
Juice ¼ lime
Juice ½ lemon
½ oz. papaya juice
2 dashes Passionola
1 oz. gin
1 oz. Myers rum
Ice

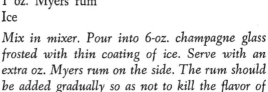

Mix in mixer. Pour into 6-oz. champagne glass frosted with thin coating of ice. Serve with an extra oz. Myers rum on the side. The rum should be added gradually so as not to kill the flavor of the drink.

DEL MONTE ELECTION DAY SPECIAL (nonalcoholic)
Courtesy, Del Monte Properties Company, Pebble Beach, California

2 dashes vinegar
1 teaspoon Worcestershire sauce
1 egg, floated
2 dashes Tabasco sauce
A little salt and pepper

Place ingredients in a sherry glass, being careful that yolk of egg does not break.

DEL MONTE LODGE COCKTAIL
Courtesy, Del Monte Properties Company, Pebble Beach, California

⅓ Kahlua cordial
⅓ brandy
⅓ heavy cream
Ice

Shake well. Strain into cocktail glass.

DELMONICO

Dash Angostura bitters
½ jigger French vermouth
½ jigger dry gin
Ice

Shake. Strain into cocktail glass. Add 2 twist orange peel.

DESERT ORANGE BLOSSOM

Courtesy, Camelback Inn, Phoenix, Arizona

Juice 1 orange
Juice 1 lemon
1 tablespoon powdered sugar
1 oz. dry gin

Shake thoroughly in shaker of chipped ice and serve well chilled. Add soda water to fill glass.

DETROIT ATHLETIC CLUB

By Walter S. Cummings, Manager, Detroit Athletic Club

1 jigger bourbon
1½ jiggers gin
1 jigger fresh lemon juice
½ jigger simple sirup
White 1 egg

Mix all ingredients and frappé.

DEWAR'S

Dash orange bitters
Dash absinthe
2 dashes grenadine
½ jigger French vermouth
1 jigger Dewar's Scotch whisky
Ice

Shake well. Strain into cocktail glass.

DEWEY

Dash Angostura bitters
½ jigger French vermouth
½ jigger Plymouth gin
Ice

Stir. Strain into cocktail glass.

DIAMONDBACK LOUNGE
Courtesy, Lord Baltimore Hotel, Baltimore

1 jigger Old Schenley rye whisky
½ jigger applejack
½ jigger yellow chartreuse
Ice

Shake well. Serve over cracked ice in old-fashioned glass. Decorate with sprig of fresh mint.

D.J.
Courtesy, Detroit Athletic Club, Detroit
"Named in honor of a former well known citizen of Detroit, D. J. Campau, who was a representative of one of Detroit's oldest families, a member of the Democratic National Committee and all that sort of thing. And he was quite a guy."

¼ grapefruit juice
¼ maraschino
¼ Italian vermouth
¼ dry gin
Ice

Shake. Serve with a hazelnut in cocktail glass.

DOMINICAN PRESIDENTE
Courtesy, Hotel Jaragua, Ciudad Trujillo, Dominican Republic

1½ oz. rum Oro
1 oz. pineapple juice
2 dashes anisette
Ice

Shake and serve in cocktail glass.

DORCHESTER OF LONDON

By Harry Craddock, American Bar, The Dorchester, London

> ¼ Bacardi rum
> ¼ Forbidden Fruit
> ½ dry gin
>
> *Stir in ice and strain into cocktail glass. Squeez
> lemon peel on top.*

DOROTHY AND DICK

By Dorothy Kilgallen and Dick Kollmar, Radio Personalities

> ½ bottle dry champagne
> ½ tumbler pineapple juice
>
> *Half fill a large pitcher with ice cubes. Pour in
> gredients over ice. Stir with long-handled spoo
> until very cold. Serve in chilled champagne glass
> with sprig of fresh mint.*

DOT-ROY

Courtesy, The Robert Treat Hotel, Newark, New Jersey

> 1 part gin
> 1 part medium sherry
> 1 part Dubonnet
> Lemon peel
> Ice
>
> *Stir. Serve in cocktail glass.*
>
> (*Note:* Use just a little less gin than sherry
> Dubonnet. This is more or less of a Dubonnet.

DOUBTING THOMAS

By Maury Machris, Beverly Hills, California

> 1 jigger (1½ oz.) white Cuban rum
> 1 jigger French cognac
> Juice ½ lime
> Juice ¼ lemon
> 1 oz. Cointreau
> ½ barspoon powdered sugar
>
> *Shake vigorously with ice. Strain and pour over
> shaved ice into large old-fashioned glass. Decorate
> with half slice of orange.*

DUGLAS FAIRBANKS

Courtesy, Sloppy Joe's Bar, Havana

⅔ gin
⅓ DuBouchett apricot brandy
Juice 1 lime
1 egg white

Shake with cracked ice, and serve in tall glass.

DRAKE

Courtesy, Hotel Drake, New York City

Juice ½ lime
⅓ Grand Marnier
⅔ brandy
Ice

Shake well. Serve in cocktail glass.

DRAKE VESUVIUS

Courtesy, The Drake, Chicago

Juice ½ lemon
1 teaspoon sugar
1 jigger orange juice
¾ jigger Gold rum
¾ jigger Jamaica rum
4 dashes red fruit coloring

Shake well and strain into 10-oz. highball glass filled with shaved ice. Decorate with fruit and sprig of mint. Place 10-oz. glass so that it rests on a cake of dry ice at bottom of a 16-oz. glass. In space between glasses pour hot water over dry ice. Use of dry ice gives a smoky effect.

DRURY'S CASA

Courtesy, Café Martin, Montreal

½ jigger rye whisky
½ jigger French vermouth
½ jigger Italian vermouth
Ice

Shake well. Strain into cocktail glass.

DRY WHISTLE
Courtesy, Lindy's, New York City

> Juice 1 small lime or ½ lemon
> ¾ light rum
> ¼ Cointreau
> Ice
>
> *Shake well and serve in cocktail glass.*

DUBONNET (chilled)

> 2 oz. Dubonnet
> Cracked ice
> Twist lemon peel
>
> *Put ice into a mixing glass and pour Dubonne over it. Stir well. Strain into cocktail glass. Add lemon peel.*

DUBONNET COCKTAIL

> ½ jigger Dubonnet
> ½ jigger dry gin
> Ice
>
> *Stir well, and strain into cocktail glass.*

DUBONNET FIZZ

> Juice ½ orange
> Juice ¼ lemon
> 1 teaspoon DuBouchett cherry brandy
> 1 glass Dubonnet
>
> *Shake well, strain into medium-sized glass (10-oz fizz or lemonade glass) and fill with soda water.*

DUBONNET ON THE ROCKS

> 1 jigger Dubonnet
> Dash of water (charged or soda)
> Cracked ice
>
> *Fill old-fashioned glass with ice. Pour in Dubon net. Add water, and twist of lemon peel, if de sired.*

DUBONNET SANGAREE

1½ jiggers Dubonnet
2 dashes Angostura bitters
¼ teaspoon sugar
1 jigger of water
Ice

Stir. Serve in wine goblet.

DUCHESS

Dash Angostura bitters
⅓ jigger absinthe
⅓ jigger French vermouth
⅓ jigger Italian vermouth
Ice

Stir. Strain into cocktail glass.

DUKE

Dash Angostura bitters
2 dashes absinthe
2 dashes anisette
1 jigger French vermouth
Ice

Stir. Strain into cocktail glass.

DU PONT HOTEL
Courtesy, Hotel du Pont, Wilmington

1¼ oz. brandy
1 oz. dry sherry
1 dash Angostura bitters
Ice

*Stir and strain into cocktail glass. Serve with twist
of orange peel.*

DUQUESNE CLUB WHISKEY SOUR
By Joe Pandl, Maitre d'Hotel, Duquesne Club, Pittsburgh

Juice ½ lemon
2 oz. rye whisky
1 teaspoon sugar
1 egg white
Ice

Shake well and serve in highball glass with no fruit.

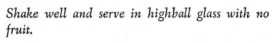

Drink today, and drown all sorrow;
You shall perhaps not do't tomorrow.

JOHN FLETCHER
(*The Bloody Brother*)

EARLY BIRD

By Hy Gardner, Columnist, New York Herald Tribune, and Radio Commentator

> 1 jigger Dubonnet
> 1 jigger dry gin
>
> *Shake and pour over the rocks in old-fashioned glass. Add twist lemon peel.*

EDGEWATER BEACH

Courtesy, Edgewater Beach Hotel, Chicago

> 1¼ oz. Jamaica rum
> ½ oz. Italian vermouth
> ¼ oz. lemon juice
> 1 teaspoon sugar
> 1 dash orange bitters
> ¼ preserved peach
>
> *Shake well with shaved ice and serve in a champagne glass.*

EGGNOG

The eggnog is a drink of American origin, particularly in the Southern states. It now enjoys world-wide popularity, especially around the Christmas and holiday season.

> 1 egg
> 1 tablespoon powdered sugar
> 1 jigger (1½ oz.) any liquor
> 1 glass of milk
>
> *All the ingredients are shaken together with ice. Serve in large highball glass, with grated nutmeg on top.*

EL MOROCCO SPECIAL NO. 2

Courtesy, John Perona

> 1 jigger Italian vermouth
> 1 jigger imported gin
> 1 dash Campari bitters
> Ice
>
> *Stir well. Strain into cocktail glass. Add twist lemon peel.*

EL MOROCCO SPECIAL NO. 3

Courtesy, John Perona

Juice ¼ lime
1 fresh pineapple stick (crushed)
1 teaspoon sugar
1 jigger Jamaica rum
1 jigger white Cuban rum
Dash curaçao
Ice

Shake well. Strain into champagne glass.

EL PRESIDENTE

1 oz. white Cuban rum
½ oz. orange curaçao
½ oz. dry vermouth
Dash grenadine
Ice

Shake well and strain into cocktail glass.

ELBOW BEACH

Courtesy, Elbow Beach, Paget, Bermuda

Juice ½ lime or lemon
1 oz. Barbados rum
½ oz. unsweetened cherry cordial
Sirup to sweeten to taste or
    maraschino cherry juice
Ice

Shake well and strain into cocktail glass.

"ELMER THE GREAT" COOLER (nonalcoholic)

By Joe E. Brown, Star of Stage, Screen and Radio

4 oz. grape juice
2 oz. orange sirup

Pour over shaved ice which fills ⅓ of a highball glass. Fill glass with club soda. Stir slightly. Decorate with orange slice, maraschino cherry, and sprig of fresh mint.

95 : *Cocktails and Mixed Drinks*

EMBASSY

Courtesy, Embassy Club, The Windsor, Montreal

½ oz. dry gin
½ oz. French vermouth
Dash Cointreau
Ice

Stir and serve in cocktail glass.

EMERALD

½ jigger Italian vermouth
½ jigger Irish whisky
Dash orange bitters
Ice

Stir. Strain into cocktail glass. Decorate with thin slice of fresh lime.

EMIL COLEMAN

By Emil Coleman, Society Orchestra Leader

½ oz. lime juice
½ oz. Falernum
1¼ oz. Bacardi rum
Ice

Shake. Strain into cocktail glass.

EMILY SHAW'S SPECIAL

Courtesy, Emily Shaw's Inn, Pound Ridge, New York

¼ lemon juice
⅛ Italian vermouth
⅛ Cointreau
½ brandy
Ice

Shake. Strain into cocktail glass.

Elysian Nymphs

By BEN STAHL

½ oz. cognac
½ oz. Grand Marnier
Champagne
Cube ice

Put ice, cognac, and Grand Marnier into a large brandy snifter. Fill glass with chilled champagne. Decorate with thin slice orange.

ERROL FLYNN RESUSCITATOR
By Errol Flynn, Motion Picture Star

Vodka
Tomato juice
Lemon juice
2 drops Tabasco
½ teaspoon Worcestershire
Ice
Salt and pepper

Take between thumb and forefinger of the right hand your largest old-fashioned glass. Half fill this with vodka, holding the glass up to the light to see if it leaks. Add half this amount of tomato juice. Now mix in a little lemon juice, the Tabasco and Worcestershire. If there is room, drop in an ice cube and, if there is still room, a couple of sprinkles of salt and pepper.

Down all this without pausing for breath, and in a few minutes, if you see a burnt matchstick on the floor, you will jump over it three feet in the air.

EVERGLADES COLLINS
By Jefferson Wynne, Miami Beach

Juice 1 lemon
1 jigger dry gin
1 jigger Cointreau
Ice

Serve in Collins glass. Fill with club soda.

EXCELSIOR SPECIAL
Courtesy, Excelsior Bar, Hotel Excelsior, Rome

2 parts sweet vermouth
1 part dry Martini vermouth
1 part Campari bitters
1 orange peel

Put ice in small tumbler, add carbonated water and serve.

97 : *Cocktails and Mixed Drinks*

EYE OPENER

½ jigger brandy
½ jigger French vermouth
2 dashes curaçao
2 dashes maraschino
2 dashes absinthe
2 dashes orange bitters
Ice

Shake well. Strain into cocktail glass. Add a cherry and twist of lemon peel.

Laugh and be merry, remember, better the world with a song,
Better the world with a blow in the teeth of a wrong.
Laugh, for the time is brief, a thread the length of a span.
Laugh and be proud to belong to the old proud pageant of man.

JOHN MASEFIELD
(*Laugh and Be Merry*)

FAIRMONT

Courtesy, Fairmont Hotel, San Francisco

½ oz. Grand Marnier
1 oz. white rum
Juice ½ lime
Ice

Shake well and strain into cocktail glass. Decorate with twist of lemon rind.

FERNET

Courtesy, Excelsior Bar, Hotel Excelsior, Rome

3 parts sweet vermouth
1 part Fernet Branca

Shake well in ice with orange peel and serve in a half tumbler or old-fashioned glass.

FITZ-G-HONEYMOONER

By Ed and Pegeen Fitzgerald, Radio and TV Personalities

1 teaspoonful honey
Juice ½ lemon
½ jigger curaçao
1 jigger white rum

Dissolve honey with lemon juice. Add curaçao, rum and ice. Shake vigorously. Strain into cocktail glass. Decorate with a thin slice of lemon.

FIVE-STAR FINAL (summer cooler)

By Inez Robb, International News Service Columnist

Ginger ale
Lemon rind
3 cubes ice
Fresh mint

Place ice in a Tom Collins glass. Cut rind of one lemon in a spiral and curl it around ice cubes in glass, with one end of rind spiral overhanging rim of glass. Add sprig fresh mint and fill glass with ginger ale.

FIZZ

Juice ½ lemon
½ teaspoon sugar
Fruit sirup
Spirits
Ice
Charged water

An effervescent drink usually made of the all ingredients. The most popular Fizzes are the Fizz, Golden Fizz, Silver Fizz, Royal Fizz, Orleans Fizz, and Whisky Fizz.

FLAMINGO

Courtesy, The Flamingo Hotel, Las Vegas, Nevada

1 oz. Cuban rum
½ oz. pineapple juice
1 dash grenadine
Juice ½ lime

Mix ingredients in electric mixer with fine Pour entire contents in saucer champagne and serve with short straws.

FLAMINGO COOLER

Courtesy, The Flamingo Hotel, Las Vegas, Nevada

1 oz. Cuban rum
1½ oz. Passionola
Juice 1 fresh lime

Mix in electric mixer with fine ice. Pour contents into tall, 14-oz. glass and fill with water.

FLIP

A drink made with liquor and sugar, mixed an egg, and spiced. Among the most popular are the Applejack, Brandy, Port, Sherry, Whisky Flips.

FRAPPE

An after-dinner drink of liqueur served in a cock-tail glass over shaved ice.

Green crème de menthe was the original Frappé. Now all liqueurs, including cognac and all the after-dinner cordials, may be served frappéed.

FRED HARVEY SOUTHWESTERN SPECIAL

Courtesy, Atchison, Topeka and Santa Fe Railway

⅔ jigger Spanish brandy
⅓ jigger Kahlua cordial
Very small dash Ojen

Shake well in mixing glass with cracked ice. Strain and serve in cocktail glass.

FREDDY MARTIN

By Freddy Martin, Orchestra Leader

¾ oz. rum
¾ oz. brandy
¾ oz. Cointreau
Juice ½ lemon

Shake with cracked ice and strain into cocktail glass.

FRENCH "75"

1 jigger gin
Juice ½ lemon
1 teaspoon sugar

Mix and pour into 14-oz. highball glass, ⅓ full of shaved ice. Fill remainder of glass with champagne.

FRENCH'S FILLIP
 By Winsor French, Columnist, Cleveland Press

> 1 egg yolk
> ½ Grand Marnier
> ¼ Courvoisier
> ¼ crème de vanilla
> Ice
>
> *Put all ingredients in shaker and shake well. Stir into large champagne glass and fill glass with fine, brut champagne, well iced.*

FROZEN SCOTCH EL BORRACHO
 Courtesy, El Borracho Restaurant, New York City

> Juice ½ lemon
> ½ teaspoon sugar
> Dash Cointreau
> Dash Angostura bitters
> 1 thin slice fresh pineapple
> 1 jigger Scotch
>
> *Place ingredients in electric mixer with shav ice. Mix well. Serve in old-fashioned glass a garnish with a thin stick of fresh pineapple.*

FULL HOUSE

> 1 dash Abbott's bitters
> ⅓ yellow chartreuse
> ⅓ benedictine
> ⅓ apple whisky
>
> *Frappé.*

FUR COLLAR
 Courtesy, The Colony Restaurant, New York City

> ⅓ orange juice
> ⅓ vodka
> ⅓ apricot brandy
> Ice
>
> *Shake and serve in cocktail glass.*

FUTURITY

½ sweet vermouth
½ sloe gin
3 dashes Angostura bitters
2 dashes grenadine

Shake well with cracked ice and strain into cocktail glass.

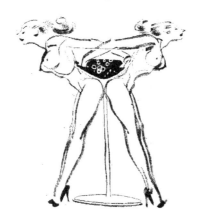

Drink no longer water, but use a little wine
for thy stomach's sake.   I Timothy 5:23

GARDEN OF ALLAH
Courtesy, The Garden of Allah, Hollywood

¼ jigger D.O.M. benedictine
¼ jigger crème de cacao
4 dashes anisette
1 egg white
1 oz. cream

Mix in shaker with shaved ice and strain into champagne glass.

GAXIOLA
By William Gaxton, Star of Stage, Screen and TV

Juice ½ lime
1 jigger (1½ oz.) Spanish brandy
2 dashes orange water
1 teaspoon powdered sugar
Ice

Shake well. Strain into cocktail glass. Decorate with thin slice of fresh lime.

GENE AHERN GLOOM CHASER
By Gene Ahern, Author of the Comic Strip "Room and Board"

2 oz. lemon juice
Sugar to sweeten, but still on sour side
2 oz. light Cuban rum
1 oz. very light Haiti rum
1 oz. Cointreau
½ oz. cognac
2 oz. cola

Stir thoroughly and pour into tall glass filled with shaved ice.

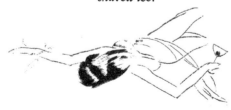

GENE TUNNEY "PUNCH"

By Gene Tunney, Retired Undefeated Heavyweight Boxing
Champion of the World

"This is a most refreshing and delightful summer drink."

1 oz. light rum
Italian Asti Spumonti champagne
1 slice green lime

Put the slice of lime on the bottom of a 6-oz.
let with a stem. Pour the rum over it. Then
goblet with shaved ice and pour the champagne
to the brim.

GENERAL BROCK

Courtesy, The General Brock, Niagara Falls, Ontario

1 oz. dry sherry
1 oz. Italian vermouth
1 oz. French vermouth
Dash Angostura bitters
Ice

Serve cold with maraschino cherry in cocktail
glass.

GEORGE OLSEN

By George Olsen, Bandleader

¼ stewed peach
¼ lime juice
¼ lemon juice
1½ oz. Southern Comfort
Shaved ice

Mix in mixer. Serve in 4-oz. glass.

GEORGES CINQ

Courtesy, Hotel Georges V, Paris

1 teaspoon lemon juice
2 dashes grenadine
⅕ apricot brandy
⅗ gin
2 drops cognac
Ice

Shake and serve in cocktail glass.

107 : *Cocktails and Mixed Drinks*

GIBSON

½ French vermouth
½ dry gin
Ice

Stir. Strain into cocktail glass. Add pearl onion.

GIMLET

1 jigger gin
Juice ½ lime

*Serve in small tumbler over cracked ice. Fill glass
with seltzer.*

GIMLET BENGAL

A British drink devised in India originally, which spread throughout the
Orient as a tropical drink.

Gin
Rose's sweetened lime juice
1 large ice cube
1 green cherry
1 thin slice fresh lime

*Chill a champagne glass thoroughly. Put in the
ice cube and pour gin over it until ice floats.
Over that, pour the lime juice (the unsweetened
will not do) to cover the surface. Add cherry and
slice of lime.*

GIN 'N' BITTERS

1½ oz. dry gin
2 dashes Angostura bitters
1 ice cube

*Put bitters in old-fashioned glass with ice. Pour
gin over all, stir and serve with stir rod.*

GIN AND TONIC (American version)

1½ oz. jigger gin
Slice lemon
Cracked ice

*Put gin and ice in 8-oz. highball glass. Fill glass
with quinine water and add lemon slice.*

GIN AND TONIC (original)

This drink originated in the tropics, but now is an international favorite

1½ oz. dry gin
Thin slice lime or lemon
2 cubes crystal-clear ice

Rub peel of fresh lime or lemon around inside edge of 8-oz. glass. Pour in gin and add ice. Add lime or lemon slice and fill glass with quinine water.

GIN COBBLER

3 oz. gin
1 teaspoon sugar

Fill wine goblet ¼ full of cracked ice. Add sugar and gin. Fill glass with water and stir well. Decorate with half a slice of orange, a maraschino cherry, and a pineapple stick.

GIN COCKTAIL

1 jigger Old Tom gin
1 dash orange bitters
Ice

Stir. Strain into cocktail glass.

GIN DAISY

Juice ½ lemon
½ teaspoon powdered sugar
6 dashes grenadine
1 jigger dry gin

Half fill a highball glass with finely cracked ice. Stir until glass is frosted. Pour ingredients over ice. Fill with soda water. Decorate with a sprig of fresh mint, a slice of lemon, and a slice of orange.

GIN FIX

1 teaspoon sugar
1 teaspoon water
1 jigger gin
½ jigger cherry brandy
Juice ½ lemon

Dissolve sugar in the water in an old-fashioned glass. Add other ingredients. Fill glass with fine ice. Stir gently. Add slice of lemon and serve with straw.

GIN FIZZ

Juice ½ lemon
1 teaspoon sugar
1 jigger dry gin

Shake well with ice. Strain into 8-oz. highball glass. Fill with soda.

GIN HIGHBALL

1 jigger gin
Cracked ice

Pour gin into highball glass over ice. Fill with charged water.

GIN OLD-FASHIONED

1 cube sugar
Dash Angostura bitters
1½ oz. gin

Muddle sugar and bitters in an old-fashioned glass with a dash of soda water. Add cracked ice, gin, and a twist of lemon peel. Stir.

GIN ON THE ROCKS

1 jigger gin
Soda water or charged water
Twist lemon peel, if desired

Fill an old-fashioned glass with cracked ice. Pour in gin, add soda water and lemon peel.

GIN RICKEY

1 jigger gin
Juice and rind ½ lime
Lump of ice

Place ingredients in 8-oz. highball glass. Fill with soda water.

GIN SANGAREE

1½ jiggers gin
2 dashes Angostura bitters
½ teaspoon sugar
1 jigger water
Ice

Stir. Serve in 8-oz. highball glass.

GIN SLING

1 lump sugar
1 teaspoon water
1 jigger gin
Piece twisted lemon peel
Lump ice

Dissolve sugar in the water in old-fashioned glass. Pour in gin. Stir. Add grated nutmeg and lemon peel, and serve with small spoon.

GIN SOUR

Juice ½ lemon
½ barspoon powdered sugar
1 jigger gin
Ice

Shake well and strain into Delmonico glass. Add dash club soda, half a slice of orange, and a cherry.

GIN TODDY

1 lump sugar
3 teaspoons water
1 jigger gin
Lump ice
Dash nutmeg

Dissolve sugar in water in an old-fashioned glass. Add ingredients. Serve with teaspoon. For a Hot Gin Toddy, leave out the ice, add hot water.

111 : *Cocktails and Mixed Drinks*

GLOOM CHASER

Juice ¼ lemon
⅓ jigger grenadine
⅓ jigger Grand Marnier
⅓ jigger curaçao
Ice

Shake well. Strain into cocktail glass.

GLORIA (nonalcoholic)

Courtesy, The Colony Restaurant, New York City
Named after Gloria Baker in 1938.

⅓ lemon juice
⅔ orgeat sirup
Ice

Shake well and serve in long parfait glass.

GOGI'S LARUE SPECIAL

Courtesy, Gogi, LaRue's Restaurant, New York City

1 split chilled champagne
1 jigger Grand Marnier
Curlicue cucumber peel
Cracked ice

Serve in silver or pewter mug.

GOLDEN DAWN (*l'aube dorée*)

Courtesy, Grosvenor House, Park Lane, London
Winner of first prize at International Cocktail Competition, London, 1930.

¼ dry gin
¼ apricot brandy
¼ Calvados (apple jack)
¼ orange juice
Ice

Shake well and strain into cocktail glass. Then add a dash or two of grenadine to give it a "Golden Dawn" appearance.

GOLDEN DAWN

By Walter A. Madigan, Beverage Editor, The Hotel Gazette

This cocktail, invented by Walter A. Madigan, well-known authority on wines and liquors, was runner-up for first prize in the International Cocktail Contest for the championship of the world, London 1939.

2 parts gin
1 part orange juice
1 part apricot brandy
Dash grenadine
Ice

Shake. Strain into cocktail glass.

GOLDEN DAWN

Courtesy, New Hotel Jefferson, St. Louis

½ jigger lime juice
1 jigger orange juice
½ jigger Jamaica rum
1 jigger bourbon whisky
1 teaspoon sugar
Ice

Place in electric mixer. Strain into hollow stemmed champagne glass which has teaspoon grenadine in bottom of stem.

GOLDEN FIZZ

Juice ½ lemon
½ teaspoon sugar
1 egg yolk
1 jigger gin
Ice

Shake, strain into 8-oz. highball glass. Fill with soda.

GOLDEN GLOW

Courtesy, New Hotel Jefferson, St. Louis

½ jigger lemon juice
1 jigger orange juice
1 teaspoon sugar
1 jigger bourbon whisky
Dash Jamaica rum

Put in electric mixer with shaved ice. Strain into hollow-stemmed champagne glass, which has stem filled with grenadine sirup.

GOLDEN SLIPPER

Courtesy, Hotel Last Frontier, Las Vegas, Nevada

"Named in honor of our new Golden Slipper Saloon and Gambling Hall, located in the Last Frontier Village."

¼ oz. cream
1 egg yolk
¾ oz. brandy
¼ oz. cherry liqueur
1 barspoon sugar
Ice

Shake, serve in cocktail glass.

GOOD-BYE

By Joan Crawford, Motion Picture Star and Winner of the Academy Award

Juice ½ lime
½ jigger vodka
½ jigger apricot brandy
Dash grenadine

Mix in electric mixer with shaved ice. Serve in champagne glass frappéed. Small twist of fresh lime peel.

GORAHEI

By Mark Barron, War Correspondent and Columnist, Associated Press

"I remember once during the Italo-Ethiopian that W. W. Chaplin, the NBC commentate the late John Whitaker of the Chicago *Dai News* and myself were up in the desert Gorahei on the campaign towards Ethiopia. was New Year's Day and Chaplin had pro moted—or, rather, 'stolen' from Marshal Graz ani's stores—a bottle of Italian brandy. We stole canvas feed bucket off the nose of an Italian arm mule and 'washed' it out with dry sand. Whitak talked Graziani's mess sergeant into appropriatir four of the precious lemons from the General supplies, also a half cup of sweet sirup.

"At the time I was having attacks of fever and was getting a ration of ice cubes twice a day from the portable field hospital units. We took Chap lin's brandy, Whitaker's lemons and sirup, and my hospital ice cubes and mixed our 'Gorah Cocktail to celebrate New Year's Day. The cock tail was rather strong, and we discussed mixing little water into the horse bucket to dilute it. But water was very scarce in that Gorahei dese region and we courageously decided to conserve our invaluable water."

GOURMET

Courtesy, Earle R. MacAusland, Publisher, Gourmet Magazine

Juice ½ lime
1 teaspoon sugar
1 jigger light Cuban or Puerto Rican rum
Ice

Shake. Take an old-fashioned glass, coat the rim with lime juice, and frost the glass by dipping the rim in fruit sugar. Place 2 cubes of ice in glass and pour mixed cocktail over them. Then float a tablespoon of Jamaica rum on top.

115 : *Cocktails and Mixed Drinks*

GRAND SLAM

By Hubie Boscowitz, International Card Expert

Juice ½ lemon
1 teaspoon sugar
1 jigger Carioca rum
½ jigger Coronet brandy
½ jigger curaçao
Dash kirschwasser
Ice

*Shake well. Strain into saucer champagne glass.
Decorate with thin slice of lemon.*

GRAND'S MARTINI

Courtesy, Grand Hotel Royal, Stockholm

⅔ Gordon gin
⅛ vermouth (sweet)
⅛ vermouth (dry)
2 drops kirschwasser
2 drops apricot brandy
Ice

Stir. Serve in cocktail glass.

GRANNY

*By Grantland Rice, Sports Columnist, New York Daily Mirror,
Bell Syndicate*

1 jigger I. W. Harper bourbon
½ jigger curacao
Juice ½ lime
Dash orange bitters
Ice

*Shake well. Strain over cracked ice into old-
fashioned glass. Add twist of orange peel.*

GRAPEFRUIT RUM BLOSSOM

1 oz. fresh grapefruit juice
1 jigger white Cuban rum
3 dashes maraschino
Ice

Shake well. Strain into cocktail glass.

Green Eyes

By RUSSELL PATTERSON

1 jigger gin
½ jigger kümmel
Ice

Shake well. Strain into cocktail glass. Decorate with green minted cherry.

GREEN STEM (after-dinner drink)

Courtesy, Trader Vic, Oakland, California

> 1 oz. cocoanut sirup
> 1 oz. white rum
> 1 oz. evaporated milk
>
> *Blend in electric mixer with fine ice. Prep*
> *chilled champagne glass by filling hollow*
> *with green crème de menthe. Place a maraschi*
> *cherry in the stem over the crème de menthe*
> *keep it from floating up into the cocoanut*
> *Then add other ingredients.*

GREEN TREE

Courtesy, Lindy's, New York City

> Juice ½ lemon
> ⅞ light rum
> ⅛ green crème de menthe
> Ice
>
> *Shake well, and serve in cocktail glass.*

GRIFF WILLIAMS MANHATTAN

By Griff Williams, Orchestra Leader

> 3 oz. bourbon
> 1 oz. Italian vermouth
> 2 dashes Angostura bitters
>
> *Stir with cracked ice and 2 good-sized pieces of*
> *cinnamon bark. Let stand for a few minutes and*
> *serve in cocktail glass. Decorate with maraschine*
> *cherry.*

GROSVENOR HOUSE

Courtesy, Grosvenor House, Park Lane, London

> ¾ jigger Gordon's gin
> ¼ French vermouth
> Dash Triple Sec Cointreau
> Ice
>
> *Mix well, and serve in cocktail glass.*

GYPSY SERENADE
By Mischa Borr, Maestro, The Waldorf-Astoria, New York City

1 jigger dry gin
½ jigger maraschino cordial
Dash orange juice
Dash lemon juice

Mix, and serve frappéed in champagne glass.

Inspiring bold John Barleycorn,
What dangers thou canst make us scorn!

ROBERT BURNS
(*Tam o'Shanter*)

HABITANT

By Larry Denis, Head Bartender, Seigniory Club, The Log Chateau, Quebec

This is a winter favorite.

2 or 3 parts rye whisky
1 part fresh lemon juice
1 part maple sirup
Dash bitters
Ice

Shake. Serve in cocktail glass.

HAMPSHIRE HOUSE

Courtesy, Hampshire House, New York City

½ oz. lime juice
½ oz. cherry maraschino juice
½ oz. Grand Marnier
2½ oz. Bacardi Cuban "Carta Blanca"
Ice

Shake. Serve in cocktail glass.

HARVARD

This drink was popular at Cambridge long before the prohibition era.

1 dash orange bitters
⅖ jigger brandy
⅗ jigger Italian vermouth
Ice

Place ingredients in old-fashioned glass over ice, stir and fill glass with club soda.

HARVEY'S

Courtesy, Harvey's Restaurant, Washington, D. C.

½ brandy
¼ gin
¼ grapefruit juice
3 dashes Cointreau
Dash orange bitters
Ice

Shake. Serve in cocktail glass.

HAVANA COCKTAIL

½ jigger apricot brandy
¼ jigger dry gin
¼ jigger Swedish punch
Dash lemon juice
Ice

Shake well. Strain into cocktail glass.

HAWAIIAN ROOM
Courtesy, Hotel Lexington, New York City

1 oz. rum
½ oz. Triple Sec
½ oz. applejack
½ oz. lemon juice
½ oz. pineapple juice

Shake with plenty of cracked ice until very cold
Strain into cocktail glass.

ST
ier, Columnist, "My New York," King Features

Gilbey's gin
Olive
Onion
2 drops Italian vermouth
2 small mint leaves

Chill a Martini glass for at least half an hour before using. Fill it with the gin, and drop in not an olive or an onion, but BOTH. Leave then in 5 minutes, then take them out. Add vermouth to gin. Float mint leaves on top of drink. Thus you have virtually pure gin tempered by the touch of vermouth and gilded by the memory of the olive and onion, and the tart presence of mint

HENRI SOULE'S SPECIAL

Courtesy, The Pavillon Restaurant, New York City

½ teaspoon fresh lemon juice
1 teaspoon powdered sugar
2½ oz. imported French cognac
2 pieces thin orange peel
Ice

Place the orange peel in a mixing glass. Add ingredients and shake well. Strain into iced cocktail glass.

HENRI SPECIAL

Courtsey, Henri's French Restaurant, New York City

½ French Calvados or apple brandy
½ French apricot brandy
A little fresh lime juice
Ice

Shake. Strain into cocktail glass.

HI, LADIES!

By Herb Sheldon, Radio Commentator, American Broadcasting Company, New York City

"Then it's ' 'Bye, Ladies!' after two drinks!"

2 oz. vodka
Juice ½ lime
½ teaspoon sugar
Few leaves fresh mint

Shake well with ice to break up the mint. Strain into cocktail glass.

HIGHBALL

1 jigger of a specified spirit
Cracked ice
Charged water

Pour liquor over ice in highball glass. Add charged water.

Today a Highball may consist of any of the popular spirits, including applejack, bourbon, brandy, gin, rum, rye, Scotch, etc. With an Applejack, Bourbon, Gin, Rum or Rye Highball, ginger ale may be used instead of soda water.

HOLLYWOOD-ROOSEVELT SPECIAL

Courtesy, Hollywood-Roosevelt Hotel, Hollywood

Dash absinthe (or absinthe substitute)
Dash Dubonnet
⅓ dry vermouth
⅔ gin
Ice

Shake. Serve in cocktail glass.

HOME STAR DUSTER

By Paul Walker, Harrisburg, Pennsylvania

1½ oz. blended rye
½ oz. apricot brandy

Stir in fine ice and serve in cocktail glass with cherry.

HOMESTEAD CLARET CUP

Courtesy, The Homestead, Hot Springs, Virginia

1 lb. fresh strawberries
4 teaspoons powdered sugar
Juice 1 lemon
1 pt. claret
1 pt. whipped cream
1 bottle soda

Crush and strain strawberries with sugar and lemon juice. Add claret, whipped cream, and soda. Mix, sweeten to taste. Serve in claret cup.

HONEST JOHN

By George Sidney, Motion Picture Director

". . . a drink with a pleasant jab and a disarming name. That dash—just a dash—of ginger ale is what gives it that nice, easy-to-take taste. Very comfortable and agreeable toward the end of a long, hot day."

2 jiggers bonded bourbon
Dash ginger ale
2 lumps ice
Twist lemon peel

Serve in old-fashioned glass. Fill with sparkling or soda water and top with twist of lemon peel.

HONEY SOUR

By Louis Sobol, Columnist, "New York Cavalcade," New York Journal-American

Juice ¾ lemon
1 level teaspoon honey
2 oz. Old Joe bourbon

Dissolve honey in lemon juice before shaking. Add ice, then shake well and serve in cocktail glass.

HONG KONG COOLER

Courtesy, The Colony Restaurant, New York City

Champagne
Fresh mint

Fill a Tom Collins glass with cracked ice. Decorate with long branches of fresh mint and fill with champagne.

HOOLEY

By James H. Barry, Jr., Tuxedo Park, New York

¼ jigger green crème de menthe
¾ jigger brandy
Ice

Blend in electric mixer. Serve in cocktail glass.

HORSE'S NECK (nonalcoholic)

Ginger ale
3 ice cubes
Rind of one lemon

Place ice in a Tom Collins glass. Cut rind lemon in spiral and curl it around ice cubes, with one end of rind spiral overhanging rim of glass Fill with ginger ale.

HOT APPLE TODDY

Courtesy, The Rabbit Club, Philadelphia

"Our custom here is to have the toddy made about seven o'clock the morning, and when we meet at one o'clock it is ready for drink ing. The toddy is served in small glasses that hold about two ounce each."

12 winesaps or pippins
12 lumps sugar
2 bottles Jamaica rum (light)
1 bottle cognac
2 qt. boiling water

Place apples in oven, with lump of sugar on each apple. Do not core them. When baked, place apples in an earthenware crock and add the rum (a light variety), cognac, and boiling water. Keep crock close to an open fire, pouring the contents of the jug back and forth from time to time, take ing care not to bruise or break the apples. The longer the crock stands before the fire, the better Great care must be exercised so that the mixture does not boil.

HOTEL ATLANTICO

Courtesy, Hotel Atlantico, Monte Estoril, Portugal

Juice ½ lemon
½ jigger brandy
½ jigger cherry brandy
Ice

Shake, and serve in cocktail glass.

HOTEL DU PARC
Courtesy, Hotel Du Parc and Majestic, Vichy, France

Juice 1 mandarin
⅓ Cointreau
⅔ jigger gin
Ice

Shake, and serve in cocktail glass.

HOTEL GAZETTE
*Courtery, Charles B. Bowne, President, The Hotel Gazette,
New York City*

⅔ Puerto Rican golden rum
⅓ fresh lemon juice
2 dashes Cointreau
Ice

Shake well. Strain into cocktail glass.

HOTEL GEORGIA
Courtesy, Hotel Georgia, Vancouver

2 parts gin
1 part orgeat sirup
½ part lemon juice
10 drops orange flower water
1 egg white (or whole egg, if preferred)

*Shake well before adding ice. This gives a nice
"top." Then add ice to chill, and serve in cocktail
glass.*

HOTEL MIRAMAR
Courtesy, Miramar, Cannes

⅓ Dubonnet
⅓ Noilly Prat vermouth
⅓ dry gin
Drop cognac
Very small zest of lemon
Ice

Shake. Serve in cocktail glass.

HOTEL NACIONAL DE CUBA

Courtesy, Hotel Nacional de Cuba, Havana

1½ oz. Bacardi rum
2 oz. pineapple juice
1 teaspoon lemon juice
1 teaspoon apricot brandy
Ice

Shake well, pour into cocktail glass and garnish with stick of pineapple and a cherry.

HOTEL REFORMA

Courtesy, Hotel Reforma, Mexico

½ oz. crème de cacao
1 oz. milk
1½ oz. cognac
Ice

Add a little cinnamon after shaking. Serve in cocktail glass.

HOTEL SASKATCHEWAN

Courtesy, Hotel Saskatchewan, Regina, Canada

Juice 1 lemon
1 barspoon liquid honey
1 jigger Canadian rye whisky
Cube ice

Stir well, and strain into cocktail glass.

HULA-HULA

1 jigger dark rum
1 jigger pineapple juice
½ jigger orange juice
½ jigger curaçao
Ice

Shake well. Strain into cocktail glass. Serve with fresh pineapple stick.

HUNTER

By Frank Hunter, "21" Brands, Inc., New York City

½ oz. Tribuno dry vermouth
1½ oz. Tribuno sweet vermouth

Pour into mixing glass with cracked ice. Twist and drop 2 orange peels into mixer. Stir rapidly, and strain into cocktail glass.

HUNTINGTON SPECIAL

Courtesy, The Huntington, Pasadena, California

Juice 1 lime
½ barspoon sugar
1 oz. pineapple juice
½ oz. crème de violette
⅕ jigger Jamaica rum
⅘ jigger brandy

Shake well with cracked ice and serve in large cocktail glass.

The brown bowle,
The merry brown bowle,
As it goes round-about-a,
  Fill
  Still,
Let the world say what it will,
And drink your fill all out-a.

The deep canne,
The merry deep canne,
As thou dost freely quaff-a,
  Sing
  Fling,
Be as merry as a king,
And sound a lusty laugh-a.

POOR ROBIN'S ALMANAC
(Old Wassail Song)

IF

By Perry Como, Singer

> 1 jigger brandy
> Dash kirschwasser
> Dash orgeat sirup
> Dash absinthe (or substitute)
> 1 teaspoon heavy cream
> Shaved ice
>
> *Blend in electric mixer. Serve in champagne glass with maraschino cherry.*

INVIGORATOR

By Piels

This drink is recommended for a cold winter night, while enjoying television by the open fireside.

> 1 bottle Piel's or Trommer's light beer
>
> *Pour beer into pewter or metal tankard. Take an iron poker and heat it in log fire until red hot. Then dip poker three or four times in the beer. Remove poker from tankard. This drink is a guaranteed "pepper-upper."*

IRISH WHISKY OLD-FASHIONED

> 1½ oz. Irish whisky
> 1 cube sugar
> Dash Angostura bitters
>
> *Muddle sugar and bitters in an old-fashioned glass with dash of soda water. Add cracked ice, whisky, and twist lemon peel. Stir.*

IT HAPPENED LAST NIGHT

By Earl Wilson, Columnist, New York Evening Post *and Post-Hall Syndicate*

> Juice ½ lemon
> ½ jigger dry gin
> 1 jigger cherry brandy
> Dash Angostura bitters
> Ice
>
> *Shake well. Strain into old-fashioned glass over cracked ice and fill with soda water.*

130 : *Bottoms Up*

"IT'S ALL NEW YORK"

By George Hamilton, Columnist

1 jigger Old Schenley bourbon
Dash orange bitters
Dash DuBouchett Triple Sec
Ice

*Shake. Strain into cocktail glass and add twist
lemon peel.*

131 : *Cocktails and Mixed Drinks*

J

When the mint is in the liquor and its
    fragrance on the glass,
It breathes a recollection that can never,
    never pass—
When the South was in the glory of a
    never-ending June,
The strings were on the banjo and the fiddle
    was in tune,
And we reveled in the plenty that we thought
    could never pass
And lingered at the julep in the ever-brimming
    glass.

CLARENCE OUSLEY
(*When the Mint Is in the Liquor*)

JACK ROSE COCKTAIL

¾ jigger applejack
¼ jigger grenadine
Juice ½ lemon
Ice

Shake well, and strain into cocktail glass.

JAMAICA RUM COBBLER

3 oz. Jamaica rum
1 teaspoon sugar
Cracked ice

Fill wine goblet ¼ full with ice. Add sugar and rum. Fill glass with water, stir well. Decorate with half a slice of orange, maraschino cherry, and pineapple stick.

JAMAICA RUM COLLINS

Juice ½ lemon
½ barspoon powdered sugar
1 jigger Jamaica rum

Shake well and strain into Collins glass. Add lump ice and fill glass with soda water.

JAMAICA RUM SOUR

Juice ½ lemon
½ barspoon powdered sugar
1 jigger Jamaica rum
Ice

Shake well and strain into Delmonico glass. Add dash club soda, half a slice of orange, and maraschino cherry.

JARAGUA PUNCH

Courtesy, Hotel Jaragua, Ciudad Trujillo, Dominican Republic

½ oz. lime juice
1 oz. orange juice
1½ oz. dark rum
3 dashes curaçao cider with grenadine
Shaved ice

Serve in large punch glass and decorate with fruit.

JOCKEY CLUB

1 dash orange bitters
1 jigger dry gin
Ice

Stir and strain into cocktail glass.

JOHN COLLINS

Juice ½ lemon
½ barspoon powdered sugar
1 jigger Holland gin

*Shake well and strain into Collins glass. Add
lump ice and fill glass with soda water.*

JOHN PERONA
Courtesy, John Perona, El Morocco's Host

1 jigger Italian vermouth
1 jigger Bacardi white rum
Dash Campari bitters
Twist orange peel
Twist lemon peel
Ice

Stir and strain into cocktail glass.

JULEPS: ANTOINE'S MINT JULEP
Courtesy, Antoine's Restaurant, New Orleans

2 oz. bonded Kentucky bourbon
1 lump sugar
4 sprigs mint

*Fill tall glass with crushed ice and set it aside. In
old-fashioned glass, crush sugar with a stick. Add
mint leaves and bruise slightly. Add whisky and
mix all together. Pour over the crushed ice in tall
glass. Stir until outside of glass is frosted. Deco
rate with large sprig of mint on top and sprinkle
with powdered sugar.*

135 : *Cocktails and Mixed Drinks*

JULEPS: ARNAUD'S MINT JULEP

Courtesy, Arnaud's Restaurant, New Orleans

Few sprigs fresh mint
1 teaspoon powdered sugar
1 jigger bottled-in-bond bourbon

Crush mint and sugar together in 8-oz. glass. Add bourbon and fill with cracked ice. Stir vigorously until glass is frosted. Decorate with sprigs of fresh mint dipped in powdered sugar.

JULEPS: BROWN HOTEL MINT JULEP

Courtesy, The Brown Hotel, Louisville

"Mint juleps may be served in a highball glass, but are much more attractive and delectable if served in silver mint-julep cups.

"Plain crushed ice may be used but mint-julep ice (flaked ice) is preferable. Make this by chipping or shaving a block of ice across the grain with a 5- or 6-prong ice chipper."

8-10 mint leaves
1 barspoon powdered (superfine) sugar, or
      1 lump sugar
½ jigger water
2½ oz. bourbon whisky

Crush (muddle) mint leaves in 10-oz. silver mint-julep cup with powdered sugar or cube sugar and water. Fill cup with crushed or flaked ice. Add bourbon and frappé vigorously until cup is frosted. Fill cup with more ice, if needed. Decorate with 4 or 5 sprigs of mint. Add slice of fruit, if desired. Serve with soda straws.

JULEPS: GREENBRIER JULEP

Courtesy, The Greenbrier and Cottages, White Sulphur Springs, West Virginia

"Legend had it that the julep originated here at The Greenbrier. W have never been able to track this one down for specific verification but we do know that it was here that the Governor of North Caro lina said to the Governor of South Carolina, 'It's a long time between drinks.' "

4 oz. bourbon
10-12 fresh mint leaves
1 level teaspoon granulated sugar

In a 14-oz. cup, muddle lightly sugar, mint leave and ½ oz. of the bourbon. Then add remainde of bourbon (3½ oz.) and fill cup ⅔ full of crushed ice. Now spoon until cup begins to frost, then add more crushed ice, filling cup solidly. Top off with 2 sprigs of mint. Shake a little confectioner's sugar over the sprigs to give it the finishing touch.

JULEPS: HENRY CLAY KENTUCKY MINT JULEP

Courtesy, Hotel Lafayette, Lexington, Kentucky

"Kentucky mint julep" of Henry Clay, given to Captain Thomas Clay, his grandson.

1 teaspoon sugar
Little water
Bourbon whisky
Mint

Gather the tender sprigs of mint in the early morning, while the dew from heaven is thick upon them. Do not let them wilt, but place them carefully in a glass of cold water in a refrigerate until ready for use, which, if I am not badly mis taken, will be before long. In making mint jule use silver cups. First, a little water and, say, a tea spoon of sugar should be put into the cup and dissolved thoroughly. Next, fill the cup with spar kling cracked ice and stir well. Now we have arrived at the most important part of concoctim a mint julep.

Pour in a liberal portion of good old bourbo whisky, let it trickle through the ice and stir we

137 : *Cocktails and Mixed Drinks*

Take a goodly number of sprigs of mint and push them down separately and very gently through the ice to the bottom of the cup, being careful not to mash or bruise them any more than can be helped. Let the mint protrude a few inches above the top of the cup.

Now the julep is ready to sample, but stop and take a long look at the frosted cup and then take a nose dive well into the mint which, after several whiffs, you will find very pleasing to the olfactory nerves. Of course, the amount of whisky and sugar must be used according to the taste. When the mint is placed in a toddy and mashed, it is a Mint Smash and not a Mint Julep.

JULEPS: HOTEL GENERAL SHELBY MINT JULEP
Courtesy, Hotel General Shelby, Bristol, Virginia-Tennessee

2 oz. bourbon
½ teaspoon sugar
4 sprigs mint

Mash mint and sugar with muddler so as to dissolve some sugar in mint juice. Add the bourbon, mixing well. Fill glass with shaved ice and allow glass to frost. Then dip rim of glass in powdered sugar. Pour in bourbon and mint juice, and stir. Add dash of rum. Decorate with sprigs of mint and serve with a straw.

JULEPS: HOWARD DAYTON HOTELS MINT JULEP
Courtesy, Howard Dayton Hotels, Albany, Georgia

12 leaves broad-leafed mint
Corn whisky or bourbon (well-aged)
Powdered sugar
Water
Apple
Shaved ice

Cover mint leaves with powdered sugar, adding sufficient water to dissolve sugar. Crush mint gently for 5 minutes, placing portion of same in bottom of a tankard, preferably of pewter or silver, al-

though stainless steel or Tom Collins glass can be used. Pack ⅔ full with shaved ice. Add remainder of mint and sugar and fill to the brim with shaved ice, packed solidly. Put tankard or glass in the refrigerator for a couple of hours. A half hour before serving, fill tankard or glass with well-aged corn whisky or bourbon. Add sprigs of mint and a couple of pieces of raw apple, sliced thin with skin removed. Serve with straw inserted on one side.

JULEPS: IRVIN S. COBB'S MINT JULEP

By the late Irvin S. Cobb, American Humorist and Writer
Courtesy, Hotel Irvin Cobb, Paducah, Kentucky

"The Irvin Cobb recipe was given to our hotel by him, and our copy bears his signature."

Mint
Bourbon
Sugar
Cracked ice

"Take from the cold spring, some water, pure the angels are; mix it with sugar till it seems like oil. Then take a glass and crush your mint in with a spoon—crush it around the border of the glass and leave no place untouched. Then throw the mint away—it is a sacrifice. Fill with cracked ice the glass; pour in the quantity of bourbo which you want. It trickles slowly through the ice. Let it have time to cool, then pour your sugared water over it. No spoon is needed, no stirring a lowed. Just let it stand a moment. Then around the brim, place sprigs of mint, so that the one who drinks may find taste and odor at one draught.

"And that, my friend, is one hell of a fine julep."

139 : *Cocktails and Mixed Drinks*

JULEPS: KOLB'S MINT JULEP
Courtesy Kolb's Restaurant, New Orleans

1½ oz. bourbon whisky
1 level teaspoon soft sugar
1 teaspoon water
10 to 12 mint leaves

Soak mint leaves in 10-oz. glass with sugar and water. DO NOT MASH them, but bruise against glass with mixing spoon. Add bourbon, then gradually keep adding fine ice. Keep pounding with mixing spoon until outside of glass shows frosting. Then fill heaping full with fine ice and decorate with about 6 sprays of mint.

JULEPS: LAFAYETTE HOTEL MINT JULEP
Courtesy, Hotel Lafayette, Lexington, Kentucky

6 to 8 sprigs mint
4 oz. Kentucky bourbon
1 teaspoon granulated sugar
4 oz. cold water
Crystal ice

Gather the mint early in the morning while the dew is on. Be careful not to bruise the mint. Set mint away in the refrigerator in a crock or glass bowl with enough water to cover stems until ready for use.

Dissolve sugar in water, then add bourbon. Fill silver cup with crystal ice. Pour ingredients over the ice. Insert gently, so as not to bruise, 6 to 8 sprigs of mint, and dive your nose into the mint. No straws, please.

For a loving cup, increase the proportion for each person.

140 : *Bottoms Up*

JULEPS: OLD ABSINTHE HOUSE MINT JULEP

Courtesy, Old Absinthe House, New Orleans

Sprigs of mint
2 oz. 100-proof bourbon
1 teaspoon sugar
½ oz. American brandy

*Press several sprigs of mint into bottom of regu
lation mint julep glass and fill glass with shaved
ice. Pour in the bourbon, add sugar and frappe
well. Then add brandy. Decorate with sprig of
mint dipped in sugar for a snowy effect, drape
mint over side of glass and serve.*

JULEPS: PARTRIDGE INN MINT JULEP

Courtesy, Partridge Inn, Augusta, Georgia

1 teaspoon sugar
1 teaspoon water
3 sprigs mint
1½ oz. bourbon whisky
1½ oz. rye whisky

*Dissolve sugar and water in 10-oz. glass. Crush 2
sprigs mint, bruise with muddler and place in
glass. Also, wipe side of glass with the fresh mint.
Fill glass half full of crushed ice, add the other
sprig of mint and completely fill glass with crushed
ice. Add bourbon whisky and rye whisky and re-
volve contents gently for a minute with long
spoon. Garnish with mint sprigs and bury in ice
until served.*

JULEPS: PATIO ROYAL MINT JULEP

Courtesy, The Patio Royal, New Orleans

1 teaspoon sugar, preferably powdered
6 sprays mint
2½ oz. rye or bourbon
½ oz. Triple Sec

*Mash mint and sugar thoroughly in a tall glass.
Add rye or bourbon and shaved ice. Stir until
glass is frosted on outside. Top with Triple Sec
and decorate with sprigs of mint, a slice of orange
and cherries. Serve with a straw.*

141 : *Cocktails and Mixed Drinks*

JULEPS: ROOSEVELT MINT JULEP

Courtesy, The Roosevelt Hotel, New Orleans

Mint
1 teaspoon granulated sugar
1 jigger whisky

The secret of making this drink is crushing mint thoroughly while mixing whole drink. Use 10-oz. glass. Drop sprig of mint in glass, add sugar, and crush mint with muddling stick made of wood. Add whisky and fill glass with crushed ice. Add a bouquet of mint and sprinkle powdered sugar on top. Serve with double straws.

JULEPS: ST. REGIS MINT JULEP

Courtesy, St. Regis Restaurants, New Orleans

2 oz. bourbon
½ teaspoon sugar
4 sprigs mint

Mash mint and sugar with muddler in tall glass. Fill glass with shaved ice, add bourbon and stir until outside of glass is frosted. Top with dash Jamaica rum. Decorate with sprigs of mint and serve with straws.

JUNIOR

By Gene Ahern, Cartoonist, Creator of "Room and Board"

2 oz. rye
1 oz. cherry brandy

Stir with cracked ice and strain into Martini glass. Add stem cherry.

Old books, old wine, old Nankin blue;—
  All things, in short, to which belong
  The charm, the grace that Time makes strong,—
All these I prize, but (*entre nous*)
            Old friends are best!

HENRY AUSTIN DOBSON
(To Richard Watson Gilder

KENTUCKY DERBY

By Bill Corum, President of Churchill Downs, and Sports Columnist,
New York Journal-American *and International News Service*

> 1 jigger Great Seal bourbon
> ½ jigger benedictine
> Ice
>
> *Shake well. Serve over cracked ice in old-fashioned glass. Add twist of lemon peel.*

KEY-LAMITY

Courtesy Yale Key, Yale University

This is strictly a winter drink to be served on cold nights only.

> 8 oz. water
> Piece cinnamon bark
> 10 or 12 whole cloves
> 1-inch piece vanilla pod
> 2 jiggers dark rum
> 1 teaspoon sugar
> ½ pat butter
>
> *Put water to boil. Add cinnamon bark, cloves and vanilla pod and boil two or three hours, until water is highly flavored and dark as coffee in color. Pour into tall glass. Add rum and sugar. Let butter melt on top and sprinkle on a little nutmeg.*

KICK IN THE PANTS

Courtesy, Olmsted's, Washington, D. C.

Originally made by Bert Olmsted in 1913 at a San Francisco restaurateurs' meeting, and has been featured at Olmsted's ever since.

> ⅓ brandy
> ⅓ bourbon
> ⅓ lemon juice
> Dash Cointreau
>
> *Shake well with ice, and serve in a chilled cocktail glass.*

KING EDWARD HOTEL

Courtesy, King Edward Hotel, Toronto

¾ Myers Jamaica rum
¼ strained lime juice
6 drops clear maple sirup

Shake well with ice, scratch a few particles of nut-meg on top and serve in cocktail glass.

KISS ME AGAIN

Courtesy, Billy Reed, The Little Club, New York City

1 jigger Scotch whisky
Dash Pernod
White 1 egg
Ice

Shake vigorously and serve in chilled champagne glass.

KNEECAP

By Eddie Buzzell, Motion Picture Director

"I used to make a drink on cold nights that I called, instead of a 'Nightcap,' a 'Kneecap'—two of 'em and you walked home on your knees."

½ bourbon
½ port wine
Ice

Shake. Serve in cocktail glass.

KOLB'S SPECIAL

Courtesy, Kolb's Restaurant, New Orleans

3 dashes cherry juice
¼ jigger dry vermouth
¾ jigger apple brandy
Twist orange peel
Ice

Stir well, add orange peel and serve in old-fashioned glass.

145 : *Cocktails and Mixed Drinks*

KOLDKURE

Courtesy, Hotel Ritz, Paris

> Rum
> 1 teaspoon grenadine
> Juice ¼ lemon
>
> *Fill cocktail glass with rum. Stir and serve.*

KUPTAIL

By Irv Kupcinet, Columnist, "Kup's Column," Chicago Sun-Times

> 3 parts gin
> 1 part Rose's lime water (sweetened)
> Dash bitters
> 1 slice lime
>
> *Serve over a cube of ice in champagne glass.*

What harm in drinking can there be,
Since punch and life so well agree?

BLACKLOCK
(*Epigram on Punch*)

LA CITADELLE

Courtesy, La Citadelle Hotel, Port au Prince, Haiti

1 jigger rum
¼ jigger whisky
¼ jigger vermouth
¼ jigger gin
¼ jigger peppermint
¼ jigger anisette
¼ jigger crème de cacao
1 jigger cream
1 egg white
¼ jigger sirup

Shake with fine ice (cracked) until shaker is frosted. Serve in champagne glass. Sprinkle top with nutmeg.

LA CREMAILLÈRE

Courtesy, La Cremaillère-à-la-Campagne, North Castle, New York

1 part cognac
1 part Amer Picon
Dash white mint
Ice

Shake well. Serve in whisky sour glass with twist of orange peel.

LA LIBERTÉ

This cocktail was originated by Edwin K. Hastings, Resident Manager of the Waldorf-Astoria, on the occasion of the maiden voyage of *La Liberté*, the reconverted *Europa*, now part of the French Line.

4 parts English gin
1 part French vermouth
Few drops Pernod
Ice

Chill cocktail glass. Pour out ice. Coat glass lightly with few drops of Pernod. Put gin and vermouth into mixer, and ice and mix. Strain into chilled cocktail glass to which a few drops of Pernod have been added. Twist of lemon peel.

LA VIE EN ROSE

Juice ¼ lemon
1 teaspoon grenadine
½ jigger dry gin
½ jigger kirschwasser
Ice

Shake well and strain into cocktail glass. Decorate with maraschino cherry.

L'AIGLON DUBARRY
By Billy Wilkerson, Hollywood

¾ oz. orange juice
½ oz. Cointreau
1½ oz. gin
1 barspoon Cherry Heering
Ice

Serve in champagne glass with twist of orange peel on top.

L'AIGLON OF CHICAGO
Courtesy, L'Aiglon Restaurant, Chicago

1 jigger cognac
½ jigger curaçao
Juice ½ lime
Dash Pernod
Ice

Shake well. Serve in cocktail glass.

LADY HOPKINS
Courtesy, Hotel Mark Hopkins, San Francisco

1 jigger Southern Comfort
⅔ jigger Passionola
Juice ½ lime

Mix well without ice. Pour into 7-oz. glass packed with shaved ice. Garnish with a cherry and mint leaves.

LADY ROBERTS

Courtesy, The Claridge Hotel, Atlantic City

⅔ Gordon gin
⅓ Cointreau
Lemon peel
Ice

Stir well. Serve in cocktail glass.

LADY'S DELIGHT

Courtesy, The Brown Palace Hotel, Denver

½ jigger gin
½ jigger grapefruit juice
1 pony grenadine
1 egg white

Frappé and serve in goblet.

LAMBS CLUB SPECIAL

Courtesy, The Lambs, New York City

1 barspoon powdered sugar
1 oz. lemon juice
1½ oz. bonded bourbon
⅓ barspoon egg white
4 dashes Pernod
Ice

Shake well and strain into Delmonico glass. Top with the Pernod.

LANAI CORDIAL (after-dinner drink)

Courtesy, Beverly Hills Hotel, California

1 oz. brandy
½ oz. Drambuie

Serve in liqueur glass.

LANDING STRIP
Courtesy, Kent House, Quebec

"One and you can take off. Two and you can fly. Three and you pancake."

⅓ dry gin
⅓ orange liqueur gin
⅓ brandy
Ice

Shake, and serve in cocktail glass.

LAST WORD
Courtesy, Detroit Athletic Club, Detroit

"This cocktail was introduced around here about thirty years ago Frank Fogarty, who was very well known in vaudeville. He was called the 'Dublin Minstrel,' and was a very fine monologue artist

¼ dry gin
¼ maraschino
¼ chartreuse
¼ lime juice
Ice

Serve in cocktail glass.

LATIN MANHATTAN
By Danton Walker, Columnist, "Broadway," New York Daily News

". . . inspired by a visit to Cuba."

⅔ rum
⅓ vermouth (½ dry and ½ sweet)

Stir well with ice and serve in cocktail glass. Add piece of lemon peel.

LAUGH TO WIN (after-dinner drink)
By Arthur Neale, Bartender, The Masquers, Hollywood

1¼ oz. green crème de menthe
1 oz. cream
Cracked ice

Put in mixing machine to crush ice, or shake very well until the ice is fine. Serve in 3-oz. cocktail glass.

151 : *Cocktails and Mixed Drinks*

LAURENTIDE INN

Courtesy, The Laurentide Inn, Ste. Agathe des Monts, Quebec

2 oz. Scotch whisky
½ oz. lemon juice
1 large teaspoon sugar
½ egg white

Add ice and shake well. Serve in cocktail glass with dash of nutmeg on top.

LAURINO

Courtesy, The Excelsior Bar, Hotel Excelsior, Rome

1 part Campari bitters
2 parts vermouth
1 slice lemon
1 slice orange

Serve in small tumbler with ice.

LE VEAU D'OR

Courtesy, Henri, Le Veau d'Or, New York City

2 parts Dubonnet
1 part kirsch
1 part lemon juice
Ice

Shake well. Strain into cocktail glass.

LE VEAU D'OR APERITIF

Courtesy, Henri, Le Veau d'Or, New York City

2 parts gin
2 parts Cinzano
1 part Campari bitters

Service in wine glass with cube of ice, and add twist lemon peel.

LEATHERNECK

By Frank Farrell, Columnist, "New York—Day by Day," New York World-Telegram and Sun, and McNaught Syndicate

"Shake violently on the rocks and serve in cocktail glass . . . Stop smoking. Fasten your seat belts. Empty your fountain pens. Because after two gulps, you seriously consider yourself capable of straight ing out Chinese fire drills."

Juice ½ lime
3 parts Four Roses rye whisky
1 part Bols Blue curaçao
Ice

Shake well. Strain into cocktail glass.

LEE LYLES SPECIAL

By the late Lee Lyles of the Santa Fe Railroad

¼ jigger orange juice
¼ jigger lemon juice
⅔ jigger dry gin
⅓ jigger French vermouth

Pour over cracked ice in mixing glass, shake we and strain into cocktail glass.

LIBERAL

Courtesy, The Colony Restaurant, New York City

¼ jigger Amer Picon
¾ jigger Old Schenley bourbon
Dash maple sirup
Ice

Stir and serve in cocktail glass. Add twist of lemon peel.

LIFE—WITH SALT ON THE SIDE

By E. V. Durling, Columnist, King Features Syndicate

2 jiggers Dewar's Scotch whisky
Dash orgeat sirup
Twist orange peel

Put cracked ice into an old-fashioned glass. Pour whisky over it. Add dash sirup and twist orange peel.

LIGHTER SIDE
By Maurice Van Metre, Columnist, Cleveland News
"Potent and cooling."

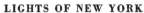

> 1 jigger rum
> 1 jigger brandy
> 1 jigger coffee
> 1 teaspoon honey
>
> *Shake well and serve in tall glass over chipped ice.*

LIGHTS OF NEW YORK
By L. L. Stevenson, Columnist, Bell Syndicate

> ½ jigger Scotch
> ¼ jigger Italian vermouth
> ¼ jigger French vermouth
> Dash Angostura bitters
> Ice
>
> *Stir. Strain into old-fashioned glass over cracked ice. Add twist of lemon peel.*

LIQUEUR D'AMOUR (after-dinner drink)
Courtesy, The Colony Restaurant, New York City

> ⅓ Pernod
> ⅓ kirschwasser
> ⅓ Anis Del Mono
>
> *Serve in cordial glass.*

LITTLE CLUB COOLER
Courtesy, Billy Reed, The Little Club, New York City

> 1 jigger Cuban rum
> ½ jigger curaçao
> Shaved ice
>
> *Serve in highball glass and fill with pineapple juice.*

Courtesy, The Little Club, New York City

"This is quite popular with the younger set. Makes a wonderful before- or after-dinner drink."

> 1 jigger Scotch
> ½ jigger Drambuie
>
> *Serve with cracked ice in an old-fashioned glass*

LITTLE CLUB NO. 2

Courtesy, The Little Club, New York City

> 1 jigger vodka
> ½ jigger Cherry Heering
> Dash lime juice
> 1 egg white
> Ice
>
> *Pour all ingredients into cocktail shaker and shake extremely well. Serve in cocktail glass.*

LITTLE KING

By Otto Soglow, Cartoonist

> Juice ¼ lemon
> ¼ jigger apricot brandy
> ¼ jigger applejack
> ½ jigger dry gin
> Ice
>
> *Shake well. Strain into cocktail glass.*

LONSDALE-HANDS PILE DRIVER

By Richard Lonsdale-Hands, British Industrial Designer

"For adults only!"

> 1 measure gin
> 1 measure sherry
> 1 measure vodka
> ¼ measure Cointreau
> Ice
>
> *Shake, and serve in old-fashioned glass.*

155 : *Cocktails and Mixed Drinks*

LOVE ME ONLY

By John P. Wilde, General Manager, The Caron Corporation

1 jigger plum or prunella brandy
½ jigger cognac
Juice ¼ lemon
Ice

Shake. Strain into cocktail glass.

LUCHOW'S SPECIAL

Courtesy, Luchow's Restaurant, New York City

"This cocktail was popular at Luchow's long before the days of prohibition."

½ oz. sweet vermouth
½ oz. dry vermouth
1½ oz. gin
1 oz. fresh orange juice

Shake well and pour into old-fashioned glass with lump of ice. Add twist orange peel and a dash of brandy or chartreuse.

LUCIUS BEEBE'S RUSSIAN RESTORER

By Lucius Beebe, Writer and Authority on Food and Drink

"This is, essentially, simply another version of a champagne cocktail, but one with which I have experienced good results, both from its therapeutic qualities and its social aspects or façade."

Champagne (preferably Bollinger or Perrier Jouet)

1 jigger strawberry brandy
Entire circular peel fresh lemon

"*Take as many very large champagne goblets as there are participants, preferably beakers holding a pint. Rub their edges with a split lime and dip in finely granulated sugar to establish a sugar coating or rim to the glass. Put brandy and the lemon peel in each glass, arranging the peel as in a Horse's Neck. Then fill to just under the sugar rim with the best vintage champagne, freezing cold. No ice cubes. Keep the entire setup so cold that no ice is necessary to the wine. There is no conceivable point in drinking champagne into which water has been permitted to intrude. Drink it while it is laughing at you.*"

LUCIUS BOOMER

*In Honor of the late Lucius Boomer, without a Doubt the Most
Eminent Hotel Operator of Our Time, and Founder and
Builder of the New Waldorf-Astoria*

(This is the recipe for an extremely dry Martini.)

Cracked ice
½ jigger dry vermouth
1 jigger House of Lords gin
1 pearl onion

*In a mixing glass, put several large pieces of cracked
ice. Pour vermouth over ice and then drain over
the vermouth, which is not used in the drink
Add gin. Stir. Strain into cocktail glass. Squeeze
lemon peel over drink, but do not drop peel into
glass. Add onion.*

Let us drink and be merry, dance, joke,
    and rejoice,
With claret and sherry, theorbo and voice!

Thomas Jordan
(*Coronemus Nos Rosis Anteque*)

M. AND ST. L

By Lucian C. Sprague, President, Minneapolis and St. Louis Railway

1 jigger old bourbon
1 jigger applejack
Dash Angostura bitters
1 barspoon Cointreau
Juice ½ lemon
Ice

Shake all ingredients vigorously and pour into old-fashioned glass over cracked ice. Decorate with twist of orange peel dropped in glass.

MAC SPECIAL

By Bill McDermott, Beverage Department Manager, Chateau Frontenac, Quebec

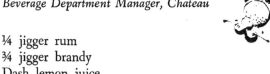

¼ jigger rum
¾ jigger brandy
Dash lemon juice
2 dashes Cointreau
Dash grenadine

Add a touch of sugar and shake with cracked ice. Serve in whisky sour glass.

MAD HATTER

Juice ¼ lemon
Juice ¼ lime
1 teaspoon powdered sugar
1 jigger Schenley Reserve whisky
Ice

Shake. Strain into cocktail glass. Add dash absinthe.

MADEIRA EGGNOG

1 egg
1 jigger (1½ oz.) Madeira
1 tablespoon powdered sugar
1 glass milk

Break egg into shaker. Add ice and ingredients. Shake well and strain into long highball glass. Grate a little nutmeg on top.

MADRID PALACE

By J. S. Brucart, Bartender, Palace Hotel, Madrid

7/10 dry gin
2/10 orange juice
1/10 Cointreau
Ice

Squeeze orange peel on top. Serve in cock glass.

MAGGI

By Maggi McNellis, Radio and TV Commentator, and One of America's Ten Best-Dressed Women

Half pony Grand Marnier liqueur
French champagne
Twist orange peel
Cube ice

Place ice in center of saucer champagne Pour in liqueur and fill with champagne, chilled. Add orange peel.

MAIDEN'S DREAM

1 jigger absinthe
1 jigger gin
1 teaspoon grenadine
Ice

Shake well. Strain into large cocktail glass. Add maraschino cherry.

MAIDEN'S PRAYER

Juice ¼ orange
Juice ¼ lemon
1 oz. Cointreau
1 oz. gin
Ice

Shake well. Strain into cocktail glass.

161 : *Cocktails and Mixed Drinks*

MAISONETTE

Courtesy, The St. Regis, New York City

Juice 1 lime
1 teaspoon sugar
2 oz. vodka
Few leaves fresh mint
Ice

Shake well, and strain into cocktail glass.

MALICE IN FOLLYWOOD NO. 1

*By Hedda Hopper, Hollywood Columnist, Chicago Tribune—
New York News Syndicate, Inc., and Radio Commentator*

"... guaranteed to open up the most secretive mind."

1 part apricot brandy
1 part bourbon
Ice

Serve in cocktail glass.

MALICE IN FOLLYWOOD NO. 2

By Hedda Hopper

"... just sample and you'll come back for more."

1 jigger rock candy sirup
2 jiggers lemon juice
3 jiggers bourbon
Ice

Shake. Serve in cocktail glass.

MANGA REVA PUNCH

Courtesy, The Surf Club, Miami Beach

"The tropical presentation of this drink adds much to its popularity
The contents blend so as to be almost indistinguishable. For years we
would offer the drink free to anyone who would tell us what the
combination was, and it was only guessed once."

1 part Triple Sec
2 parts lime juice
5 parts apple and honey

*Shake well and pour 3 oz. into a cocoanut shelf
sawed off at the top to a 2½-inch opening and the
kernel removed. Fill rest of cocoanut with finely
cracked ice, stir once, and close opening with
square slice of fresh pineapple into whose side
pineapple top leaves have been attached. Mount
this cocoanut on a ring of fresh pineapple so that
it will not tumble. Garnish with sea grape or galax
leaves, and serve with brightly colored, cellophane
straws.*

MANHATTAN (dry)

⅓ French vermouth
⅔ rye whisky
Ice

*Stir. Strain into cocktail glass. Add maraschino
cherry.*

MANHATTAN (sweet)

The Manhattan is a preprohibition cocktail, and the original recipe called
for dash orange bitters. Today bitters are not used.

⅓ jigger Italian vermouth
⅔ jigger rye whisky
Ice

*Stir well. Strain into cocktail glass. Decorate with
maraschino cherry.*

163 : *Cocktails and Mixed Drinks*

MANHATTAN NOONDAY

Courtesy, Noonday Club, St. Louis

> 1½ oz. bourbon whisky
> Dash bar sirup
> Dash Angostura bitters
> 1 oz. Italian vermouth
>
> *Stir in cocktail shaker with ice. Strain into cocktail glass, and serve with a cherry.*

MARCO

Courtesy, The Colony Restaurant, New York City

> 1 jigger gin
> Dash Angostura bitters
> Dash simple sirup
> Dash lime juice
> Ice
>
> *Shake well, and serve in cocktail glass.*

MARQUISETTE

Courtesy, Restaurant Marguery, New York City

> 1 oz. Cuban rum
> 1 oz. imported gin
> Juice ½ lime
> 1 tablespoon grenadine
>
> *Sugar the rim of the glass. Put in cube of ice and shake. Serve in cocktail glass, with little slice of lime on top.*

MARTIN CASA

Courtesy, Café Martin, Montreal

> Juice ½ lime
> ½ oz. apricot brandy
> ½ oz. Cointreau
> 2 oz. Jamaica rum
> Ice
>
> *Serve in cocktail glass.*

MARTINI

Many recipes are in use in making Martinis today. This is the original recipe of this preprohibition cocktail.

Dash orange bitters
½ jigger Old Tom gin
½ jigger Italian vermouth

Stir (do not shake). Strain into cocktail glass containing small green pitted olive.

MARTINI (dry)

⅔ dry gin
⅓ jigger Noilly Prat vermouth
Ice

Stir. Strain into cocktail glass which has small green pitted olive or lemon twist, according to taste. Some Martini fanciers prefer a small pickled pearl onion instead of lemon twist or olive.

MARTINI (extra dry)

For a very dry Martini, increase the gin proportion and reduce the vermouth.

⅘ dry gin
⅕ French vermouth
Ice

Stir. Strain into cocktail glass. Add twist of lemon peel.

MARTINI (sweet)

½ jigger Italian vermouth
½ jigger gin

Some Martini drinkers prefer a sweet Martini. For this drink, use Italian, or sweet, vermouth instead of French, or dry, vermouth.

MASQUERS BLOODY MARY

By Arthur Neale, Bartender, The Masquers, Hollywood
"Great after a tough night!"

8 oz. tomato juice
1¼ jiggers tequila
1 teaspoon Worcestershire sauce
Juice ½ lime
3 drops Tabasco

Pour over ice cubes in 10-oz. highball glass. Fill glass with tomato juice, season with salt and pepper, stir and serve.

MAXIM'S OF PARIS

Courtesy, Louis Vaudable, Owner of Maxim's Restaurant, Paris

Dry French champagne
1 lump sugar
2 brandied cherries

Place cherries in a large saucer champagne glass. (Do not use maraschino cherries.) Crush cherries with sugar. Fill glass with champagne, well chilled.

MAYFAIR

Courtesy, The Claridge Hotel, Atlantic City

⅓ cherry brandy
⅔ gin
2 dashes grenadine
½ fresh lime
Ice

Shake well, and strain into cocktail glass.

MAYFLOWER

Courtesy, The Mayflower, Washington, D. C.

¾ oz. crème de cacao
⅓ oz. dry vermouth
⅓ oz. sweet vermouth
1 oz. dry gin

Stir well in shaker with ice. Twist lemon peel over empty cocktail glass and put in a hazelnut. Strain ingredients into glass.

Merry Widow

By John Falter

½ Dubonnet
½ French vermouth
Ice

Shake well, strain into cocktail glass. Decorate with maraschino cherry.

METEOR

By Harry Craddock, American Bar, The Dorchester, London

½ rye or bourbon whisky
¼ Italian vermouth
¼ absinthe (or absinthe substitute)
Ice

Serve in cocktail glass.

METROPOLE

This cocktail was originated at the turn of the century at the Metro Bar on West Forty-Third Street off Broadway.

Dash Peychaud bitters
Dash orange bitters
½ jigger French vermouth
½ jigger brandy
Ice

Stir. Strain into cocktail glass. Decorate maraschino cherry.

METROPOLITAN CLUB SPECIAL

Courtesy, Metropolitan Club, New York City

Juice 1 lime
1 barspoon sugar
1½ oz. Bacardi white rum
1 oz. Gordon gin
2 or 3 fresh mint leaves
Ice

Shake well, and strain into a saucer champagne glass.

MEURICE

Courtesy, Hotel Meurice, Paris

⅔ vodka
⅙ Bols crème de banane
⅕ fresh cream

Fill shaker with large pieces of clear ice and shake extremely well. Serve in cocktail glass.

MIDNIGHT ALARM

Courtesy, Parker House, Boston

1½ oz. light rum
Juice ½ lemon
1 level teaspoon sugar
2 oz. pineapple juice

Shake vigorously with ice, and serve in wine glass.

MIKE ROMANOFF

Courtesy, Romanoff's, Beverly Hills, California

1 jigger vodka
1 barspoon curaçao
1 barspoon apricot liqueur
Juice 1 lime

Shake well with cracked ice, and serve in 3-oz. glass.

MILK PUNCH

1 jigger brandy
1 teaspoon sugar
1 glass milk
Ice

Shake well. Strain into 8-oz. highball glass and serve with nutmeg on top.

MIMI

Courtesy, Hotel Georges V, Paris

1 teaspoon lemon juice
2 dashes grenadine
⅕ apricot brandy
⅗ gin
2 drops cognac
1 egg white

Rub rim of small wine glass with slice of lemon. Dip edge into powdered sugar. Shake ingredients with ice, and strain into glass.

MINT JULEP (see Juleps)

MINT SMASH

Courtesy, Kolb's Restaurant, New Orleans

½ lump sugar
A little water
6 to 8 mint leaves
1½ oz. bourbon

Dissolve sugar in water in an old-fashioned glass
Add mint leaves and mash thoroughly with mi
dler. Add medium-sized cracked ice and bourbo
Stir well.

MISS AMERICA

Courtesy, Hackney's Restaurant, Atlantic City

½ jigger bourbon from Kentucky
½ jigger applejack from New Jersey
Juice ½ lemon from California
1 barspoon sugar from Louisiana
1 barspoon grenadine from New York
1 barspoon fresh cream from Pennsylvania
Ice

Shake well, and serve in cocktail glass.

MISSED PUTT

By H. I. ("Hi") Phillips, Columnist, "The Sun Dial," New York
World-Telegram and Sun

". . . throw away your golf clubs!"

⅓ jigger grape juice
⅔ jigger Old Schenley rye whisky
Dash absinthe (or absinthe substitute)

Shake well with cracked ice, strain into cocktail
glass.

MIST

By Milton Widder, Columnist, Cleveland Press

1 jigger Southern Comfort
Juice ¼ lime

Fill old-fashioned glass with crushed ice. Pour
liquid and juice over ice. Use no sweetening
Drink through a short straw.

169 : *Cocktails and Mixed Drinks*

MISTY QUEEN

By Juan Parades, Bartender, Bellerive Country Club, Normandy, Missouri

> 1¼ oz. brandy
> Dash dry vermouth
> Dash Cointreau
>
> *Fill 6-oz. toddy glass with crushed ice. Add twist of lemon peel and serve with a straw.*

MOCAMBO

Courtesy, Charley Morrison, Hollywood

> 2 jiggers white rum
> 1 jigger gin
> 2 jiggers pineapple juice
> Ice
>
> *Shake well. Serve in cocktail glass.*

MOJITO

Courtesy, The Colony Restaurant, New York City

> Juice and rind ½ lime
> 1 teaspoon sugar
> 2 oz. rum
>
> *Serve in highball glass with 2 ice cubes. Fill with soda water and top with sprigs of mint.*

MONT TREMBLANT SPECIAL

Courtesy, Mont Tremblant Lodge, Mont Tremblant, Quebec

> Juice ½ lemon
> ⅔ apricot brandy
> ⅓ dry gin
> Ice
>
> *Shake, and serve in cocktail glass.*

MONTE CARLO CASINO SPECIAL
Courtesy, Monte Carlo Casino, Monte Carlo

Champagne
3 dashes brandy
1 teaspoon Demerara sugar, liberally soaked
    real French absinthe
Slice orange
Ice cube

*Put ingredients into champagne glass and fill
with champagne.*

MOONLIGHT AND ROSES
By Lanny Ross, Singer

"This is not too beautiful so that you can't drink it . . . and it
make you sing!"

Gin
Dash lemon juice
Grenadine
Small amount sugar
Shaved ice
Sprig mint

*Place mint in bottom of highball glass and make
it with sugar. Chill glass, and fill it solid with
shaved ice. Pour in gin to within inch of top. Add
lemon juice. Mix grenadine and sugar together
point where sugar has absorbed the grenadine
Then pour this on top of gin and ice.*

MOREHOUSE MOLLIFIER
By Ward Morehouse, Columnist, New York World-Telegram and Sun

Juice ½ lime
1 jigger vodka
½ jigger Grand Marnier
Dash orange flower water
Ice

Shake well. Serve in cocktail glass.

171 : *Cocktails and Mixed Drinks*

MORNING AFTER

By Joe Pandl, Maître d'Hôtel, Duquesne Club, Pittsburgh

2 oz. French brandy
¾ oz. Italian vermouth
Ice

Stir well, and serve in wine glass.

MORNING GLORY

Courtesy, Restaurant Marguery, New York City

2 oz. brandy
2 oz. Amontillado sherry
1 egg yolk
1 teaspoon sugar

Frappé, and serve in cocktail glass.

MORNING GLORY FIZZ

Juice ½ lemon
½ teaspoon sugar
White 1 egg
2 dashes absinthe
1 jigger Dewar's Scotch whisky
Ice

Shake. Strain into fizz or 8-oz. highball glass. Fill with club soda.

MOSCOW MULE

Courtesy, The Cock 'n Bull, Hollywood

"The Moscow Mule (now fairly famous throughout the nation) originated over the bar of my small pub in 1941, shortly before Pearl Harbor."

1 jigger Smirnoff vodka
Cock 'n Bull ginger beer
Cracked ice
½ fresh lime

Place ice in copper or earthen mug. Pour vodka over it, then fill with ginger beer. Squeeze lime for juice, then use as garnish.

MOTHER'S RUIN

By Allen Prescott, Radio and TV Commentator

"... my favorite, when I'm strong enough to take it. I have called 'Mother's Ruin' for years, but I have known it to serve as many wandering boy's one-way ticket, too."

4 parts gin
1 part French vermouth
Dash Pernod
Ice

Serve very cold in cocktail glass.

MOUNT ROYAL PUNCH

Courtesy, Mount Royal Hotel, Montreal

1 oz. curaçao
1 oz. gin
Juice 1 orange
1 egg yolk
Sugar to taste
Ice

Shake well, and serve in 12-oz. glass. Fill with ginger ale and stir before serving.

MR. AND MRS.

By Walter Kiernan, Radio Commentator

"My wife christened it 'Mr. and Mrs.' because it looks good to and there's a little left over for 'Mr.' "

2 jiggers Schenley Reserve rye
½ jigger lemon juice
½ jigger grenadine
1 egg white

Shake well with cracked ice, and strain into cocktail glasses. (This makes two cocktails.)

173 : *Cocktails and Mixed Drinks*

MR. SOULE SPECIAL

Courtesy, Le Pavillon, New York City

3 oz. imported brandy
2 dashes orange bitters
½ teaspoon powdered sugar
3 good-sized orange peels
Ice

Shake well, and strain into well-chilled cocktail glass.

MRS. MINIVER

In Honor of Greer Garson, MGM Screen Star

¼ jigger dry gin
¼ jigger cognac
¼ jigger crème de cacao
¼ jigger heavy cream
Ice

Shake vigorously, and strain into cocktail glass.

MYRTLE BANK SPECIAL

Courtesy, Myrtle Bank Hotel, Kingston, Jamaica

½ gin
¼ Italian vermouth
¼ fresh pineapple juice

Shake in mixing glass with cracked ice, and strain into cocktail glass.

A bumper of good liquor
Will end a contest quicker
Then justice, judge, or vicar.

RICHARD BRINSLEY SHERIDAN
(*The Duenna*)

NANETTE

Courtesy, Hotel Drake, New York City

½ gin
½ Aperitivo Rosso

Stir in cocktail mixer, and serve in whisky-sour glass, with small ice cube and orange peel.

NATE GROSS

Courtesy, Stockyards Inn, Chicago
Named in Honor of the Chicago Columist.

Champagne
1 jigger gin
Lump sugar
Dash orange bitters
Crushed ice

Pour gin into 12-oz. highball glass. Add sugar, bitters, ice. Fill glass with champagne. Decorate with thin slice of lemon.

NEGRONE (Italian apéritif)

Courtesy, Restaurant Marguery, New York City

1 jigger Seager's imported gin
1 jigger sweet Martini Rossi vermouth
1 jigger Campari bitters
Ice

Stir, and serve very cold in cocktail glass. Add twist lime peel.

NEGRONI CAPRICCIO

Courtesy, Capriccio Restaurant, Rome

⅓ Gordon gin
⅓ Campari bitters
⅓ Cinzano vermouth (sweet)

Finish with a little seltzer, and serve in an old-fashioned glass with a lot of ice. Add twist orange peel.

NEGRONI DONEY

Courtesy, Doney Veneto Restaurant, Rome

⅓ jigger Doney gin
⅔ jigger Doney bitters
¼ jigger Carpano vermouth
½ slice orange

Serve with soda and ice in cocktail glass.

NEGRONI-RITZ OF PARIS

By Georges, The Ritz Bar, Paris

¼ jigger dry gin
½ jigger Italian vermouth
¼ jigger Campari bitters
Dash Angostura bitters
Ice

Shake well. Strain into old-fashioned glass with lump ice, half slice orange, half slice lemon maraschino cherry.

NEW ORLEANS FIZZ

Courtesy, Sloppy Joe's Bar, Havana

½ part gin
½ part cream
1 teaspoon sugar
1 egg white
2 drops kirsch

Shake with ice, and serve in tall glass.

NEW ORLEANS GIN FIZZ

1 jigger dry gin
1 egg white
6 drops orange flower water
2 oz. sweet cream
Juice 1 lemon
1 teaspoon sugar

Shake extremely well with ice. Strain and pour into 10-oz. highball glass. Fill glass with soda.

NEW WALDORF

As prepared at the new Waldorf-Astoria.

½ House of Lords gin
¼ French vermouth
¼ Italian vermouth
¼ slice pineapple, crushed
Ice

Shake well, and strain into cocktail glass.

NEW YORK ATHLETIC CLUB

Courtesy, New York Athletic Club, New York City

⅔ gin
⅓ dry vermouth
⅓ sweet vermouth
Ice

Shake well. Serve in cocktail glass with slice orange and slice fresh pineapple.

NEW YORK CAVALCADE

By Louis Sobol, New York Journal-American *and Syndicated Columnist*

1½ oz. white Cuban rum
1 oz. Grand Marnier liqueur
1 teaspoon grenadine
Juice ½ lemon

Mix in electric mixer, to which has been added 1 jigger shaved ice. Serve in champagne glass, ice and all, before ice has entirely melted.

NICK KENNY SPEAKING

By Nick Kenny, Song Writer and Radio Editor of New York Daily Mirror

1 jigger Irish whisky
½ jigger Triple Sec
Dash orange bitters
Ice

Shake well. Strain into cocktail glass in which has been placed a green minted cherry.

NICKY Q SPECIAL

Courtesy, El Borracho's, New York City

½ oz. lime juice
½ oz. pineapple juice
½ barspoon sugar
1 oz. gin
1 dash Cointreau

Pour ingredients in an electric mixer with fine ice. Serve in cocktail glass.

NOLA

By Vincent Lopez, Orchestra Leader

2 oz. Carioca rum
½ jigger raspberry cordial
½ jigger strawberry cordial
Juice ½ lime
Ice

Shake well. Serve frappéed in champagne glass with twist lime peel.

NOT FOR EXPORT

Courtesy, Maison Prunier, London

This recipe, by the cocktail barman of Maison Prunier of London, won third prize in the International Cocktail Competition, 1948.

⅔ Seager's gin
⅓ Seager's curaçao
1 teaspoon Drambuie
Dash lemon juice
Ice

Shake well, and serve in cocktail glass.

Live while you live, the epicure would say,
And seize the pleasures of the present day. . . .

PHILIP DODDRIDGE
(*Epigram on His Family Arms*)

OCCIDENTAL

Courtesy, Occidental Hotel, Washington, D. C.

2 oz. brandy
¼ oz. white mint
¼ oz. grenadine
2 dashes lime juice

Shake with fine ice. Strain, and serve in champagne glass.

OF THEE I SING, BABY

By William Gaxton, Star of Stage, Screen and TV

1½ oz. Jamaica rum
½ oz. Cointreau
½ oz. grenadine
Juice ½ lemon
Ice

Shake well. Strain into cocktail glass. Decorate with maraschino cherry and small sprig fresh mint.

OLD-FASHIONEDS

1½ oz. liquor desired
Cube sugar
Dash Angostura bitters
Dash soda water
Cracked ice
Twist lemon peel

The original old-fashioned cocktail is of preprohibition origin, and is made of either rye or bourbon. Place sugar in old-fashioned glass, add bitters and soda water. Muddle. Add ice, liquor and lemon peel.

During prohibition, it became the custom to decorate cocktails more profusely, so a half slice of orange and a maraschino cherry were added to the old-fashioned. Some also include a stick of fresh pineapple. Today, all types of old-fashioneds are popular, being made of applejack, bourbon, brandy, gin, Irish whisky, rum, rye, Scotch, and vermouth.

OLD JOE SOUR

By Charles Berns, "21" Brands, Inc., New York City

2 oz. Old Joe bonded bourbon
Juice ½ lime
½ teaspoon honey

Dissolve honey in lime juice and add bourbon. Shake well with ice, and strain into Delmonico glass. Squirt dash of soda water on top, and garnish with slice of orange and a cherry.

OLD ROMAGNA

Courtesy, The Excelsior Bar, Hotel Excelsior, Rome

2 parts Old Romagna cognac
1 part aurum
1 part lemon juice
Few dashes grenadine

Shake well in ice. Serve in cocktail glass.

OLD SCHENLEY EGGNOG

1½ oz. Old Schenley bonded bourbon
   or rye whisky
1 egg
1 tablespoon powdered sugar
1 glass milk

Break egg into shaker. Add ice and ingredients. Shake well, and strain into long highball glass. Grate a little nutmeg on top.

OLMSTED SPECIAL

Courtesy, Olmsted's, Washington, D. C.

Fifty years ago, in honor of the opening of Olmsted's, Bert Olmsted initiated this cocktail and it was served gratis to all guests dining there during the first months of its establishment.

½ gin
½ dry sherry
Dash Cointreau

Shake well with ice, and serve in cocktail glass.

183 : *Cocktails and Mixed Drinks*

OLYMPIC

Courtesy, Hotel Ritz, Paris

½ brandy
¼ curaçao
¼ orange juice
Ice

Shake well, and serve in cocktail glass.

OMAR'S DELIGHT

Courtesy, Omar Khayyam's, San Francisco

1 jigger (100-proof) Southern Comfort
3 dashes curaçao
Juice ½ small lime
⅓ oz. lemon juice
½ level teaspoon sugar
Fine ice to chill

Shake, or mix in electric mixer. Strain, and serve in champagne glass.

"ON THE LINE"

By Bob Considine, Columnist, International News Service

Scotch
2 lumps ice
Twist lemon peel

Take large old-fashioned glass and drop ice into it. With the free hand, lift the nearest bottle of good Scotch and pour in a double jolt. Over this intricate mixture please twist a bit of lemon peel. Drink.

ON THE ROCKS

1½ oz. liquor
Dash water plain or soda
Cracked ice
Twist of lemon peel, if desired

Fill old-fashioned glass with ice. Pour in liquor, add water and lemon peel. (Liquor may be applejack, bourbon, brandy, gin, rum, rye, Scotch or vodka.)

OPEN HOUSE

Courtesy, Zebra Room, The Town House, Los Angeles

⅔ white rum
⅓ pineapple and orange juice
2 or 3 dashes apricot brandy

Shake well with cracked ice. Serve in cocktail glass.

ORANGE BLOSSOM (original)

1 jigger dry gin
Juice ½ orange
Ice

Shake well, and strain into cocktail glass.

ORANGE BLOSSOM (speakeasy version)

½ jigger dry gin
¼ jigger Italian vermouth
¼ jigger Cointreau
Ice

Shake well. Strain into cocktail glass. Add maraschino cherry.

OSSIFIER

By Rube Goldberg, Cartoonist

1 jigger gin
1 jigger vodka
1 teaspoon Grand Marnier
Ice

Shake well. Pour into cocktail glass with twist of lemon peel.

185 : *Cocktails and Mixed Drinks*

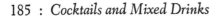

P

Nothing equals the joy of the drinker, except
the joy of the wine in being drunk.

ANONYMOUS

(Quoted by Maurice des Ombiaux: *Nouveau Manuel
de l'Amateur de Bourgoyne*)

PADDLIN' MADELINE HOME

By William Gaxton, Star of Stage, Screen and TV

1 jigger applejack
1 egg white
1 teaspoon grenadine
1 teaspoon Triple Sec
Juice ¼ lemon
Ice

Shake well. Strain into cocktail glass. Add thin slice lemon.

PALACE HOTEL

Courtesy, The Palace Hotel, San Francisco

½ brandy
½ Italian vermouth
Dash curaçao
Ice

Serve in cocktail glass. Add lemon peel.

PALACE ST. MORITZ SPECIAL

By Gustave Doebeli, Palace Hotel, St. Moritz

⅖ curaçao
⅖ Gordon's gin
1/10 lemon juice
1/10 orange juice
Dash absinthe (or absinthe substitute)
Ice

Shake well. Serve in cocktail glass.

PALMERETTE

Courtesy, Palmer House, Chicago

1 jigger white rum
Juice ½ lime
1 barspoon green curaçao
Ice

Shake and strain into cocktail glass.

PARKER HOUSE PUNCH

Courtesy, Parker House, Boston

1½ oz. New England rum
½ oz. brandy
¾ oz. cold tea
1½ oz. lemon juice
¾ oz. simple sirup
Dash seltzer water

Serve in highball or punch glass with shaved ice
Add slice orange, slice lemon and a cherry.

PASSION

⅓ jigger Coronet brandy
⅓ jigger Schenley gin
⅓ jigger green chartreuse
Few drops Amer Picon
Few drops absinthe
Ice

Shake well. Serve frappéed in champagne glass

PAUL'S OWN

By B. Paul, Head Barman, American Bar, Grosvenor House, London
Awarded first prize (by proxy) at the International Cocktail Com
petition in Vienna, 1927.

3 dashes Fernet Branca
⅓ dry gin
⅓ French vermouth
⅙ Cointreau
⅙ curaçao
Ice

Shake well and strain into cocktail glass.

189 : *Cocktails and Mixed Drinks*

PAVILLON SPECIAL

Courtesy, Le Pavillon, New York City

1 oz. gin
½ oz. French vermouth
½ oz. Italian vermouth
½ oz. cherry brandy
½ oz. kirsch
2 dashes orange bitters
Ice

Stir, cool well, and strain into chilled cocktail glass, with a cherry. Twist an orange peel on top.

PEACOCK ALLEY

As served at the old Waldorf-Astoria.

⅔ Charleston rum
⅓ maple sirup
Juice ½ lime
Ice

Shake well, and strain into cocktail glass.

PEACOCK GALLERY

As prepared at the new Waldorf-Astoria.

1 jigger Cordon Bleu brandy
Dash absinthe (or absinthe substitute)
2 dashes Abbott's bitters

Frappé. Serve in cocktail glass.

PEBBLE BEACH COMBER

Courtesy, Del Monte Properties Company, Pebble Beach, California
"A witch's brew."

1 jigger Grand Marnier brandy
Juice ½ orange
Ice

Shake well. Serve in champagne glass.

PERFECT

⅓ dry gin
⅓ French vermouth
⅓ Italian vermouth
Ice

Shake well. Strain into cocktail glass.

PERFECT LADY

By Sidney Cox, Grosvenor House, London

This cocktail was awarded first prize at the British Empire Cocktail Competition in London, 1936.

½ dry gin
¼ peach brandy
¼ fresh lemon juice
1 teaspoon egg white
Ice

Shake well, and strain into slightly larger than ordinary cocktail glass.

PERNOD DRIP

1 oz. (1 liqueur glass) Pernod
1 cube sugar

Place sugar in bottom of drip glass. Fill drip saucer with ice. Pour Pernod over ice and let drip for a few minutes. Fill glass with water over ice in drip saucer.

PHILIPPE OF THE WALDORF

Courtesy, Claude C. Philippe, Host of The Waldorf-Astoria, New York City

French dry champagne
2 dashes Vieille Cure liqueur
Dash imported French kirsch

Shake kirsch and liqueur into a large saucer champagne glass. Fill glass with champagne, well chilled. (No ice or sugar is used in the glass.)

PHOTO FINISH

By Robert G. Johnson, President, Maywood Park Trotting Association, Chicago

1 jigger Carioca rum
½ jigger curaçao
Juice ½ lime
Ice

Shake well. Strain over cracked ice in old-fashioned glass. Decorate with twist of lime peel.

PIDGE

In Honor of Walter Pidgeon, MGM Motion Picture Star

1 jigger brandy
1 dash kirschwasser
Juice ½ lemon
1 teaspoon honey
Ice

Dissolve honey in lemon juice. Then add other ingredients and ice. Shake well. Strain into cocktail glass. Add twist lemon peel.

PINE ROOM PIPPEN

Courtesy, The Carolina Hotel, Pinehurst, North Carolina

1 jigger Scotch
½ oz. Dubonnet
Dash Angostura bitters
Juice ½ lemon
¼ teaspoon sugar
Ice

Shake well. Serve in cocktail glass.

PINEAPPLE FLIP (nonalcoholic)

By Lowell Redelings, Columnist, Hollywood Citizen-News

1 egg
1 teaspoon sugar
½ cup pineapple juice
Chopped ice

Mix thoroughly, in a liquidizer, and serve in a cooled glass.

Piccadilly Circus

By GILBERT BUNDY

1 jigger dry gin
⅓ jigger French vermouth
Dash absinthe
Dash grenadine
Ice

Shake well. Strain into a cocktail glass.

PINK DEATH

By Robert C. Ruark, Columnist, New York World-Telegram and Sun

1 oz. light Cuban rum
1 oz. 151-proof rum
1 teaspoon Cointreau
Dash lime juice
¼ peach (fresh or preserved)
Ice

Mix in electric mixer and serve in double cocktail glass. Decorate with maraschino cherry.

PINK LADY

1 jigger Plymouth gin
2 teaspoons grenadine
1 egg white
Ice

Shake well and strain into cocktail glass.

PINO PEPE

Courtesy, Trader Vic's, Oakland, California

2 oz. white rum
¼ oz. maraschino liqueur
2 oz. pineapple juice
Juice ½ lime
Dash rock candy sirup

Put in electric mixer with shaved ice. Mix a few seconds and serve in a hollowed fresh pineapple. Replace top of pineapple. Serve with 2 straws.

PISCO SOUR

1 jigger Pisco brandy
Juice ½ lemon
1 teaspoon sugar
1 egg white
Ice

Shake well. Strain into Delmonico glass.

193 : *Cocktails and Mixed Drinks*

PLANTERS PUNCH

1 jigger Jamaica rum
Juice 1 lime
Shaved ice

Half fill a tall highball glass with the ice. Pour rum and lime juice over it. Add orange slice, pineapple stick and maraschino cherry. Fill glass with soda water. Serve with straws.

POLO LOUNGE

Courtesy, Beverly Hills Hotel, Beverly Hills, California

½ oz. Bacardi rum
½ oz. apricot brandy
½ oz. Amer Picon

Serve in Tom Collins glass filled with shaved ice and decorate with slice of apple.

POP LEONARD'S SPECIAL GIMLET

By Robert Z. Leonard, Motion Picture Director

1½ jiggers gin
⅛ jigger Rose's or Virginia Dare lime juice
2 dashes white crème de menthe
1 barspoon sugar or equivalent of simple sirup

Do not shake. Stir and serve in large cocktail or wine glass. Add cube ice, a green or red maraschino cherry. Garnish edge of glass with half slice lemon. Top off with dash orange flower water.

PORT COBBLER

3 oz. port
¼ teaspoon sugar
Cracked ice

Fill wine goblet ¼ full of ice. Add sugar and port. Fill glass with water. Stir well. Decorate with half slice orange, pineapple stick and maraschino cherry.

Plum Blossoms

By JOHN LA GATTA

½ jigger dry gin
½ jigger plum or prunelle brandy
1 barspoon grenadine
Juice ½ lemon
Ice

Shake well. Strain into cocktail glass. Decorate with 2 small rose petals.

PORT EGGNOG

1 jigger port wine
1 egg
1 teaspoon sugar
½ pint milk

Put into shaker with ice and shake well. Strain into 12-oz. goblet. Top with grated nutmeg.

PORT FLIP

1 jigger port
½ teaspoon sugar
1 whole egg
Ice

Shake, strain. Pour into 8-oz. highball glass. Grate nutmeg on top.

PORT WINE SANGAREE

1½ jiggers port wine
2 dashes Angostura bitters
¼ teaspoon sugar
1 jigger water
Ice

Stir. Serve in fizz glass.

POUSSE-CAFE WALDORF (after-dinner drink)
As concocted at the old Waldorf-Astoria.

⅐ raspberry sirup
⅐ anisette
⅐ Parfait d'Amour
⅐ crème Yvette
⅐ yellow chartreuse
⅐ green chartreuse
⅐ Cordon Bleu brandy

Pour carefully into a sherry glass in order given.

195 : *Cocktails and Mixed Drinks*

POWERHOUSE

By Jimmy Powers, Sports Columnist, New York Daily News—
Chicago Tribune *Syndicate, and TV Sports Commentator*

1 jigger applejack
½ jigger cherry brandy
Ice

Shake well. Strain into cocktail glass, and add twist lemon peel.

PRAIRIE OYSTER

"Morning after" pick-me-up.

Whole yolk 1 egg
2 dashes vinegar
1 teaspoon Worcestershire sauce
1 teaspoon tomato catsup
Dash pepper on top

Place ingredients in a sherry glass, being careful not to break egg yolk.

PRESIDENTE

1 jigger Bacardi rum
½ jigger French vermouth
Dash grenadine
Ice

Shake well. Strain into cocktail glass. Add twist orange peel and maraschino cherry.

PREVIEW

In Honor of Peter Lawford, Motion Picture Star.

1 jigger Schenley gin
⅓ jigger Cointreau
Dash absinthe
Ice

Shake well and strain into cocktail glass.

PRIMAVERA

Courtesy, Hotel Drake, New York City

> 1 jigger Bacardi white rum
> Juice 1 cube pineapple
> Juice ½ lime
> 1 teaspoon sugar
> Dash Cointreau
> Fresh mint leaves
> Ice

Mix in electric mixer, then strain into whisky sour glass. This is a special summer drink.

PRINCE FERDINAND

By Arnaud Cazenave, Arnaud's Restaurant, New Orleans

> ⅓ gin
> ⅓ cognac
> ⅓ French vermouth
> Few dashes lemon juice
> 1 teaspoon grenadine
> Ice

Shake and serve in a cocktail glass with a cherry.

PRINCESS

Courtesy, Princess Lounge, Royal York Hotel, Toronto

> ½ oz. Ronrico rum
> ¾ oz. lemon juice
> ¾ oz. honey

Dissolve honey in lemon juice before adding rum. Shake with chipped ice and strain into gin sour glass.

PRINCETON

> ⅔ dry gin
> Dash orange bitters

Serve in Delmonico glass. Add ice. Stir, and fill with club soda.

PRINCETON CLUB SPECIAL

Courtesy, Princeton Club of New York

2 oz. gin
½ oz. dry vermouth
½ oz. Dubonnet
Ice

Stir well, drain into cocktail glass, and add twist lemon peel.

PRUNIER

Courtesy, Maison Prunier, London

⅓ whisky
⅓ curaçao
⅓ Italian vermouth
Ice

Stir, and serve in cocktail glass.

PUMP ROOM BATH CURE NO. 1

Courtesy, Pump Room, Ambassador East, Chicago

2 jiggers 151-proof rum
1 jigger vodka
1 jigger lemon juice
3 oz. milk
Dash grenadine
1 teaspoon sugar
Ice

Shake and strain into Collins glass.

PUMP ROOM BATH CURE NO. 2

Courtesy, Pump Room, Ambassador East, Chicago

The Bath Cure has been a feature drink of the Pump Room, whose menus it is listed with the following notation: "Only on served to a guest."

1 jigger Jamaica rum
1 jigger light rum
1 jigger lemon juice
1 teaspoon sugar
3 dashes grenadine
Add milk

Shake well with finely cracked ice. Serve in 14-on glass, which is encased in ice mold packed with cracked ice, giving a perfect ice form which, in turn, is sprinkled with dashes of green and re coloring. Decorate with fruit, and float a very little Jamaica rum on top. This makes the finishe drink not only a palatable and delicious one, most attractive-looking.

PUMP ROOM SPECIAL

Courtesy, Pump Room, Ambassador East, Chicago

1½ oz. vodka
½ oz. white crème de menthe
½ oz. cognac

Frappé with shaved ice. Serve in old-fashioned glass.

PUNCH

A drink usually mixed in a bowl in large quantiy and served from the buffet in cups or glasses. . punch may also be mixed and served in an ind vidual glass. Care should be taken to mix ingred ents in such a way that neither the sweet, the bitter, the spirits, or any other liquor is more ap parent than another.

Among the most popular punches are the Mil Brandy, Champagne, Claret, Claret and Sautern Planters, Rum and Sherry Punches.

So I'm for drinking honestly, and dying in my boots.

JOHN MASEFIELD
(*Captain Stratton's Fancy*)

"RADIENT" GLOW

By Radie Harris, Hollywood Columnist and Radio Commentator

2 jiggers light rum
Dry champagne
Dash fresh lime juice
Cracked ice

Serve in Collins glass, and fill glass with dry champagne.

RAINBOW (after-dinner cooler)

By Ted Saucier

This is a delicious after-dinner drink. The glass will become frosted almost instantaneously and the effect will be that of a beautiful rain bow.

1 pony Bols Blue curaçao
1 pony yellow chartreuse
1 pony strawberry cordial
Finely shaved ice

Fill ⅓ of 10-oz. highball glass with ice. Pack firmly. Pour curaçao over it. Over curaçao pack another ⅓ glass ice, and pour chartreuse. Fill remainder of glass with ice, and pour the cordial over it. Serve with 2 straws.

RAMOS GIN FIZZ

Courtesy, Seymour Weiss, President, The Roosevelt Hotel, New Orleans

"This is the original 'Ramos Gin Fizz' recipe, as created by the first Ramos of Spanish origin years ago in his bar, now long out of existence, located on Gravier Street, facing one of the sides of the old St. Charles Hotel. Although Gin Fizzes are made everywhere in New Orleans, The Roosevelt Hotel only has the right to the name 'Ramos Gin Fizz,' bought from the heirs of the originators."

1 jigger sweet gin
3 dashes lime juice
3 dashes lemon juice
1 tablespoon powdered sugar
½ white of egg
3 dashes orange flower water
3 oz. milk or cream
Ice

Shake well. Add dash seltzer water, when completed. Serve in fizz or lemonade glass.

Red Head

By BRADSHAW CRANDELL

1 jigger Schenley Reserve
1 barspoon kirschwasser
1 barspoon raspberry cordial or sirup
Juice ½ lemon
Ice

Shake well. Strain into cocktail glass. Drop twist orange peel into glass.

RANCHO LA VISTA

By Reese L. Milner, Beverly Hills, California

"One reclines in a large easy chair and, after a time, drifts into peaceful state of oblivion. Amen."

1 jigger lemon juice
1 jigger lime juice
½ jigger Falernum
2 teaspoons honey
2 jiggers light Bacardi rum
2 jiggers dark Lemon Hart rum
2 jiggers Havana Club rum
1 jigger Myers rum
Cracked ice
Large orange peel

Use a large 14-oz. Collins glass, or a big bran snifter-type glass, half filled with the ice. The in a cocktail shaker or electric mixer, put the lime and lemon juice, honey and Falernum. When this is well mixed together, add the light, to dark, and the Havana Club rum. Mix for one minute, then pour over the ice in the large gla with the Myers rum added for a float. Place orange peel in glass and add straws.

RED LION

Courtesy, Grosvenor House, London

First prize winner in London, 1933; invented by Arthur Tarling the Café Royal.

⅓ Booth's dry gin
⅓ Grand Marnier
⅙ orange juice
⅙ lemon juice
Ice

Shake well. Moisten outside rim of cocktail glass with lemon or orange, and dip into soft sugar make a frosted edge. Strain into glass.

203 : *Cocktails and Mixed Drinks*

REMSEN COOLER

1 jigger Old Tom gin
2 cubes ice
Whole peel of lemon cut in spiral

Place in Collins glass, and fill with club soda.

RENDEZVOUS

Courtesy, Hotel Muehlebach, Kansas City, Missouri

1⅛ oz. Schenley gin
½ oz. maraschino
Juice ½ lime
Ice

Shake, and serve in cocktail glass.

RHAPSODY

By Paul Whiteman, King of Jazz, and Director of Music, American Broadcasting Company

1 jigger dry gin
⅓ jigger yellow chartreuse
Dash orange bitters
Ice

Shake well. Strain into cocktail glass. Decorate with maraschino cherry.

RICKEY

Spirits
Juice and rind half lime
Ice

Use any liquor desired. Serve in a tumbler or tall glass, with lime. Add ice and charged water.

RICKEY MADRIGUERA

By Enric Madriguera, Orchestra Leader

2 parts Jamaica rum
1 part anisette
Lemon peel
Ice

Shake. Serve in cocktail glass

Reverie

By PHIL DORMONT

1 jigger dry gin
½ jigger Marie Brizard Apry
Juice ¼ lemon
Dash kirschwasser
Ice

Shake well. Strain into cocktail glass.

RITZ OF LONDON
Courtesy, Ritz Hotel, London

½ Gordon's gin
¼ lemon juice
¼ French vermouth
Dash orange bitters
Few grains sugar
Ice

Shake well, and serve in cocktail glass.

RITZ OF MADRID
Courtesy, Hotel Ritz, Madrid

1 jigger Triple Sec liqueur
Juice ¾ lemon
Juice ½ orange
Small teaspoon sugar
Ice

Blend in electric mixer. Serve in cocktail glass.

RITZ OF PARIS
Courtesy, C. A. Auzello, General Manager, Hotel Ritz, Paris

½ jigger brandy
⅙ jigger Cointreau
Juice ¼ orange
Champagne

Shake well. Strain ingredients (except champagne) into champagne glass, until half full. Fill glass with chilled champagne.

ROB ROY

½ jigger King's Ransom Scotch
½ jigger Italian vermouth
Dash Angostura bitters
Ice

Stir, and strain into cocktail glass.

205 : *Cocktails and Mixed Drinks*

ROBERT TREAT SPECIAL
Courtesy, The Robert Treat Hotel, Newark, New Jersey

½ brandy
½ Dubonnet
Dash orange bitters
Ice

Serve in cocktail glass. Add lemon peel.

ROCK AND RYE

1 jigger rye whisky
2 teaspoons rock candy sirup

Serve in whisky glass.

ROCK GARDEN
By John P. Wilde, General Manager, The Caron Corporation

French champagne
3 or 4 pieces cracked ice

Have champagne well chilled. Put ice in old-fashioned glass and fill glass with champagne. Decorate with slice orange, fresh pineapple stick, maraschino cherry, and green minted cherry.

ROMAN PUNCH

1 jigger Jamaica rum
½ jigger brandy
¼ jigger curaçao
Juice ½ lemon
2 teaspoons sugar
2 teaspoons raspberry sirup
Port wine

Shake well all ingredients except port. Pour over shaved ice in highball glass. Decorate with fresh fruit and a port wine float on top.

ROMANOFF'S OF BEVERLY HILLS

Courtesy, Romanoff's, Beverly Hills, California

1 jigger gin
¼ jigger Cherry Heering
Dash grenadine
Juice 1 lime

Leave ½ of lime in a 12- or 14-oz. glass. Add crushed ice and ingredients, and fill glass with ginger beer.

ROOM AND BOARD

By Gene Ahern, Cartoonist

3 oz. old Jamaica rum
¾ oz. Bellows Falernum

Pour liquor over ice cube in old-fashioned glass, and decorate with orange slice and lemon peel.

ROOSEVELT

Courtesy, The Roosevelt, New Orleans

1 jigger rye whisky
1 teaspoon simple sirup
Dash Angostura bitters
Dash J. & W. bitters

Mix in glass with ice cube. Stir thoroughly. Drain into a second glass, in which has been put a dash of absinthe, or absinthe substitute, such as Herbsaint.

ROVER

By Jim O'Connor, Amusement Editor, New York Journal-American

1 jigger bonded bourbon
Lemon peel
Shaved ice

Pour liquor into old-fashioned glass. Add lemon peel and ice.

ROYAL CANADIAN

By Guy Lombardo, Orchestra Leader

1 jigger Canadian Club whisky
2 teaspoons maple sirup
Juice ½ lemon
Ice

Shake well. Strain into cocktail glass.

ROYAL FIZZ

1 jigger gin
½ teaspoon sugar
Juice ½ lemon
1 whole egg
Ice

*Shake well, strain into fizz or 8-oz. highball glass.
Fill glass with soda water.*

ROYAL HAWAIIAN

Courtesy, Moana Hotel, Honolulu

1 jigger gin
1 jigger pineapple juice
⅓ jigger lemon juice
1 teaspoon orgeat sirup
Ice

Shake well, and serve in chilled champagne glass.

ROYAL MONCEAU

Courtesy, Royal Monceau Hotel, Paris

¾ gin
¼ liqueur Suze
¼ lemon juice
Ice

Shake and serve in cocktail glass.

ROYAL YORK SPECIAL

Courtesy, Royal York Hotel, Toronto

1½ oz. dry gin
½ oz. Cointreau
Dash lemon juice
Dash grapefruit juice

Shake with cracked ice, and serve in cocktail glass.

RUBAN BLEU

Courtesy, Le Ruban Bleu, New York City

1 jigger Carioca rum
2 dashes crème Yvette
Juice ½ lemon
Ice

Shake well. Strain into cocktail glass.

RUBY FIZZ

1 jigger claret
2 dashes absinthe
Juice ½ lemon
½ teaspoon of sugar
White 1 egg
Ice

Shake. Strain into fizz or 8-oz. highball glass. Fill with club soda.

RUM AND COLA

1 jigger white rum
Juice ½ lime
Cola
Cracked ice

Pour rum and lime juice over ice in highball glass. Fill glass with cola.

RUM COLLINS

1 jigger rum
Juice ½ lemon
½ barspoon powdered sugar

Shake well, and strain into Collins glass. Add lump ice, and fill glass with soda water.

RUM DAISY

1 jigger white Cuban rum
Juice ½ lemon
6 dashes grenadine
½ teaspoon powdered sugar

Half fill a highball glass with finely cracked ice. Stir until glass is frosted. Pour ingredients over ice. Fill with soda water. Decorate with sprig fresh mint, slice lemon, and slice orange.

RUM EGGNOG

1 jigger light or dark rum
1 egg
1 teaspoon sugar
½ pint milk

Put into shaker with ice and shake well. Strain into 12-oz. goblet. Top with grated nutmeg.

RUM FIX

1 jigger rum
½ jigger cherry brandy
Juice ½ lemon
1 teaspoon sugar
1 teaspoon water

Dissolve sugar in the water in old-fashioned glass. Fill glass with fine ice. Add ingredients. Stir gently. Add slice lemon, and serve with straw.

RUM FIZZ

1 jigger Carioca rum
2 dashes absinthe
Juice ½ lemon
½ teaspoon sugar
White 1 egg
Ice

Shake. Strain into fizz or 8-oz. highball glass. Fill with club soda.

RUM JUBILEE (frozen)

By Gene Leone, Leone Restaurant, New York City

> 1 oz. Myers rum
> 2 scoops orange sherbet
> ½ scoop chocolate ice cream
> ½ oz. Myers rum float
> 2 dashes Cherry Heering
>
> *Mix sherbet, ice cream and rum with spoon. Pour in champagne glass. Add rum float and Cherry Heering.*

RUM OLD-FASHIONED

> 1½ oz. rum
> 1 cube sugar
> Dash Angostura bitters
>
> *Muddle sugar and bitters in old-fashioned glass with dash soda water. Add cracked ice, rum and twist lemon peel. Stir. Decorate with half slice orange, stick fresh pineapple, and maraschino cherry, if desired. This last is optional.*

RUM PUNCH

> 1 jigger white Cuban rum
> Juice ½ lemon
> 1 teaspoon sugar
>
> *Put ingredients in a tall highball glass. Fill glass with shaved ice. Add soda water. Decorate with orange slice, pineapple stick and maraschino cherry. Serve with straws.*

RUM RICKEY

> 1 jigger white Cuban rum
> Juice and rind ½ lime
> Lump ice
>
> *Fill with soda water. Serve in tall glass.*

211 : *Cocktails and Mixed Drinks*

RUM SLING

1 jigger rum
Lump sugar
1 teaspoon water
Twist lemon peel
Lump ice

Dissolve sugar in water. Add ingredients. Stir. Add grated nutmeg, and serve with small spoon in whisky glass.

RUM SOUR

1 jigger white Cuban rum
½ teaspoon sugar
Juice ½ lemon
Ice

Shake well. Strain into Delmonico glass. Dash siphon. Decorate with half orange slice.

RUM TODDY

1 jigger Goddard's Rum
Lump sugar
3 teaspoons water
Lump ice
Dash nutmeg

Dissolve sugar in water in old-fashioned glass. Add rum, ice, nutmeg. Serve with teaspoon. For Hot Rum Toddy, leave out ice and add hot water.

RYE DAISY

1 jigger rye whisky
Juice ½ lemon
½ teaspoon powdered sugar
6 dashes grenadine

Half fill a highball glass with finely cracked ice. Stir until glass is frosted. Pour ingredients over ice. Fill with soda water. Decorate with sprig fresh mint, slice lemon and slice orange.

RYE EGGNOG

1 jigger rye
1 egg
1 teaspoon sugar
½ pint milk

Put in shaker with ice and shake well. Strain into 12-oz. goblet. Top with grated nutmeg.

RYE OLD-FASHIONED

1½ oz. rye
Cube sugar
Dash Angostura bitters

Muddle sugar and bitters in old-fashioned glass with dash soda water. Add cracked ice, rye, and twist lemon peel. Stir.

RYE RICKEY

1 jigger rye whisky
Juice and rind ½ lime
Lump ice

Fill with soda water. Serve in tall glass.

RYE SLING

1 jigger rye whisky
Lump sugar
1 teaspoon water
Piece twisted lemon peel
Lump ice

Stir. Add grated nutmeg, and serve with small spoon in whisky glass.

RYE SMASH

1 jigger rye whisky
½ teaspoon sugar
2 teaspoons water
3 sprigs fresh mint
Cracked ice

Place mint, sugar and water in old-fashioned glass. Muddle carefully. Add whisky and ice. Serve with small spoon.

RYE SOUR

1 jigger rye
Juice ½ lemon
½ barspoon powdered sugar
Ice

Shake well and strain into whisky sour glass. Add dash club soda, half slice orange, and maraschino cherry.

RYE TODDY

1 jigger rye
Lump sugar
3 teaspoons water
Lump ice
Dash nutmeg

In an old-fashioned glass place sugar, dissolved in water. Add rye, ice, nutmeg. Serve with teaspoon. For Hot Rye Toddy, leave out ice and add hot water.

RYE WHISKY COBBLER

3 oz. rye whisky
1 teaspoon sugar
Cracked ice

Fill wine goblet ¼ full ice. Add sugar and whisky, and fill glass with water. Stir well. Decorate with half slice orange, pineapple stick, and maraschino cherry.

RYE WHISKY COLLINS

1 jigger rye whisky
½ barspoon powdered sugar
Juice ½ lemon

Shake well, and strain into Collins glass. Add lump ice, and fill glass with soda water.

Oh, 'tis jesting, dancing, drinking
Spins the heavy world around.

A. E. HOUSMAN
(*A Shropshire Lad*)

ST. CHARLES
Courtesy, The St. Charles Hotel, New Orleans

1 jigger rye whisky
Small lump sugar or 1 teaspoon simple sirup
Dash Angostura bitters
Dash Peychaud's bitters

Mix in old-fashioned glass with 2 lumps ice. Stir about 10 times. Chill a second glass, put in 2 or 3 dashes absinthe, or absinthe substitute, roll in hands, empty over sink, letting absinthe drip out of glass. Then pour in mixture and squeeze small piece lemon peel on top.

ST. FRANCIS BRANDY OLD-FASHIONED
Courtesy, Hotel St. Francis, San Francisco

1¼ oz. California brandy
½ cube sugar
2 drops Angostura bitters
½ oz. seltzer

Crush sugar and bitters together. Add brandy, seltzer and cube ice. Decorate with twist lemon peel, add maraschino cherry and stir. Serve in old-fashioned glass.

ST. FRANCIS SPECIAL MARTINI
Courtesy, Hotel St. Francis, San Francisco

> 3 parts Old Tom gin
> 1 part Noilly Prat vermouth
> Twist lemon peel
> Ice
>
> *Stir and serve in chilled glass. Decorate with hazelnut olive.*

ST. REGIS HOTEL
Courtesy, The St. Regis, New York City

> 2 oz. Barbados rum
> Juice 1 lime
> 1 teaspoon sugar
> Ice
>
> *Shake well, and pour into cocktail glass.*

STE. ADELE LODGE BLUE DIVER
By Paul Thibodeau, The Alpine, Quebec

> ¾ jigger dry gin
> ¼ jigger Cointreau or Triple Sec
> 1 oz. blue curaçao
> Juice ½ lemon
> Dash brandy
>
> *Cover bottom of glass shaker with simple sirup, add ingredients with cracked ice. Shake well, and strain into champagne glass. Add green cherry.*

SALOME

> ½ jigger Dubonnet
> ½ jigger Italian vermouth
> 2 dashes absinthe
> Ice
>
> *Stir. Strain into cocktail glass.*

217 : *Cocktails and Mixed Drinks*

SANGAREE

½ jigger sloe gin
½ jigger French vermouth
Dash phosphate
3 dashes Angostura bitters

A drink made of wine and sugar, served in a small bar glass with ice, and topped with grated nutmeg; or red wine and water, spiced and sugared. Fill fizz glass with ice.

SANGRIA (Mexican drink)
By Tex McCrary and Jinx Falkenburg, Radio and TV Commentators

1 glass (4 oz.) claret wine
1 glass (4 oz.) pineapple juice
Dash lemon juice
Sugar to taste

Place in 12-oz. highball glass with crushed ice, and fill with 2-oz. soda water. Measure wine and juice as desired, but use plenty.

SANTA FE COOLER
Originated by the late Lee Lyles of the Sante Fe Railroad

1 jigger applejack
¼ jigger DuBouchett curaçao
¼ jigger Cointreau
Juice 1 lime
Ice

Shake well. Pour into Tom Collins glass. Add cracked ice and fill glass with champagne.

SAPPHIRE
In Honor of "Skipper" Robert L. Huffines, Jr., Greenwich, Connecticut

½ jigger dry gin
½ jigger Bols Blue curaçao
2 teaspoons heavy cream
Cracked ice

Shake well. Strain into cocktail glass.

SAUTERNE COBBLER

3 oz. sauterne
¼ teaspoon sugar
Cracked ice

*Fill wine goblet ¼ full with cracked ice. Add
sugar and sauterne, and fill goblet with water.
Stir well. Decorate with half slice orange, pineapple stick, and maraschino cherry.*

SAVOY HOTEL (after-dinner drink)
Courtesy, Savoy Hotel, London

⅓ crème de cacao
⅓ benedictine
⅓ brandy

*Pour carefully into liqueur glass so the ingredi-
ents do not mix.*

SAVOY HOTEL SPECIAL NO. 1
Courtesy, Savoy Hotel, London

⅔ dry gin
⅓ French vermouth
Dash absinthe
2 dashes grenadine
Ice

*Shake well, and strain into cocktail glass. Twist
lemon peel on top.*

SAVOY HOTEL SPECIAL NO. 2
Courtesy, Savoy Hotel, London

⅔ Plymouth gin
⅓ French vermouth
2 dashes Dubonnet
Ice

*Shake well, and strain into cocktail glass. Twist
orange peel on top.*

SAVOY-PLAZA

Courtesy, Savoy-Plaza Hotel, New York City

½ Jamaica or Charleston-type rum
¼ apricot brandy
¼ lemon juice
Ice

Shake well, stir, and serve in cocktail glass.

SAVOY TANGO

Courtesy, Savoy Hotel, London

½ sloe gin
½ applejack or Calvados
Ice

Shake well, and strain into cocktail glass.

SAZERAC COCKTAIL

Original Recipe, Courtesy, Seymour Weiss, President, The Roosevelt Hotel, New Orleans

It is said that this popular and potent drink was named after a famous and fiery personality of an early period, Captain Sazerac.

Fill 1 sazerac glass with crushed ice; or put in refrigerator freeze compartment. The sazerac glass is a large old-fashioned glass nearly 4 inches high and holds 9 oz. It is made of thick glass, so as to retain the coldness when chilled. This is the glass in which to serve the finished drink.

Into a second sazerac glass put 1 small lump of sugar and then add:

2 dashes Angostura bitters
3 dashes sazerac bitters

Crush sugar with muddler. Add 2 or 3 ice cubes, over which pour 1¼ oz. straight rye whisky, 90-proof. Stir with barspoon until mixed thoroughly and cold.

Now take the first sazerac glass, empty the crushed ice, and put in 4 or 5 dashes of Herbsaint. (Herbsaint is an absinthe substitute without the wormwood.) Twirl the glass several times, so the Herbsaint will cover the entire inside of the glass. Turn upside down and shake out any remaining. At this point, take the other glass with mixture in it and flip out the ice cubes, then pour into the chilled glass, being careful not to touch the sides of the glass. Twist thin piece lemon peel over the glass, but do not put in the drink.

SCHENLEY

Juice ½ lemon
½ jigger Triple Sec
1 jigger Schenley Reserve
1 barspoon grenadine
Shaved ice

Mix in electric mixer and serve frappéed in cocktail glass. Decorate with thin slice lemon.

SCOOP

By Jack Gaver, Columnist, United Press

½ jigger applejack
½ jigger brandy
½ jigger Carioca rum
Dash apricot brandy
2 teaspoons grenadine
Ice

Shake well. Strain into double cocktail glass with shaved ice. Decorate with sprig fresh mint.

SCORPION (for four)

Courtesy, Trader Vic's Trading Post, Oakland, California

1 oz. Pisco brandy
10 oz. Ron Merito or Brugal rum
4 oz. lemon juice
2 oz. orange juice
2 oz. orgeat

Mix thoroughly, and pour over cracked ice. Garnish with fresh gardenias. Serve in a large bowl with 4 long straws.

SCOTCH OLD-FASHIONED

 1½ oz. Scotch
 Dash Angostura bitters
 Cube sugar

Muddle sugar and bitters in old-fashioned glass with dash soda water. Add cracked ice, Scotch and twist lemon peel. Stir. Decorate with half slice orange, maraschino cherry and, if desired, stick pineapple. This is optional.

SEA ISLAND

Courtesy, The Cloister, Sea Island, Georgia

 ½ oz. dry vermouth
 ½ oz. grenadine
 ½ oz. apricot brandy
 1½ oz. Van der Hum
 Ice

Stir, and serve in cocktail glass.

SEIGNIORY CLUB SPECIAL

By Larry Denis, Head Bartender, Seigniory Club, Quebec

 1½ oz. rye whisky
 1 oz. grapefruit juice
 1 teaspoon maple sirup
 Dash rum
 ½ egg white
 Ice

Shake well. Serve in cocktail glass.

SEPTEMBER MORN

 1 jigger white Cuban rum
 Juice ½ lime
 White 1 egg
 Dash grenadine
 Ice

Shake well. Strain into claret glass.

SESQUI

Courtesy, Olmsted's, Washington, D. C.

Concocted by James Brahms in honor of the Sesquicentennial.

⅓ brandy
⅓ Aquavit
⅓ Canadian Club
2 dashes crème de violette

Shake well with ice, and serve in cocktail glass.

SHADOW, THE

By Ray Schindler, Head of the Private Detective Agency

1 jigger applejack
1 jigger Coronet brandy
Juice ¼ lemon
Juice ¼ lime
Juice ¼ orange
1 barspoon grenadine
Ice

Shake well. Strain into cocktail glass.

SHANDYGAFF

This is an old, popular drink of preprohibition days.

Piel's or Trommer's light beer
Ginger ale

In a large highball glass, pour half a bottle chilled ginger ale, and half a bottle chilled beer. (No ice.)

SHERMAN BILLINGSLEY SPECIAL

Courtesy, The Stork Club, New York City

½ cherry brandy
¼ Triple Sec
¼ peach brandy
Juice 1 lime

Serve in tall glass with shaved ice.

SHERRY COBBLER

3 oz. sherry
¼ teaspoon sugar

Fill wine goblet ¼ full cracked ice. Add sugar and sherry, and fill goblet with water. Stir well. Decorate with half slice orange, pineapple stick, and maraschino cherry.

SHERRY EGGNOG

1 jigger sherry
1 teaspoon sugar
1 egg
½ pint milk

Put into shaker with ice and shake well. Strain into 12-oz. goblet. Top with grated nutmeg.

SHERRY FLIP

1 jigger sherry
½ teaspoon sugar
1 whole egg
Ice

Shake, strain. Pour into fizz glass. Grate nutmeg on top.

SHERRY-NETHERLAND

Courtesy, The Sherry-Netherland, New York City

1 jigger white rum
Juice ½ lime
½ jigger canned pineapple juice
Little powdered sugar
Couple mint leaves
Ice

Shake, and strain into a chilled cocktail glass.

SHERRY ON THE ROCKS

1½ oz. sherry
Twist lemon peel
Cracked ice

Fill an old-fashioned glass with the ice. Pour in sherry. Add water and, if desired, lemon peel.

SHERRY PUNCH

1 jigger sherry
1 teaspoon sugar
Juice ½ lemon
Shaved ice

Place sherry, lemon juice and sugar in a tall high ball glass. Fill with shaved ice. Add soda water and decorate with orange slice, pineapple stick and maraschino cherry. Serve with straws.

SHERRY SANGAREE

1½ jiggers sherry
2 dashes Angostura bitters
¼ teaspoon sugar
1 jigger water
Ice

Stir. Serve in fizz glass.

SIDECAR

⅓ DuBouchett Cointreau
⅓ Coronet cognac
⅓ lemon juice
Ice

Shake well and strain into cocktail glass.

SIDNEY FIELDS

By Sidney Fields, Columnist, "Only Human," New York Daily Mirror
"As a predinner delight, it's painless but potent."

2 parts dry sherry
1 part gin
Ice

Shake. Serve in cocktail glass.

SILVER FIZZ

1 jigger gin
Juice ½ lemon
½ teaspoon sugar
White 1 egg
Ice

Shake, strain. Fill fizz glass with soda.

SILVERMINE TAVERN RUM MINT OLD-FASHIONED
Courtesy, The Silvermine Tavern, Norwalk, Connecticut

> 1 jigger light rum
> Juice ½ lemon
> 1 teaspoon white crème de menthe
> 3 dashes curaçao
> Sugar optional
> Sprigs mint

Prepare an old-fashioned glass by muddling sprig of mint in its bottom, and rubbing the rim with crushed mint. Then discard the mint. Put ingredients in shaker and shake vigorously. Pour into the prepared glass. Add 2 ice cubes. Decorate with sprig of mint speared through green cherry.

SIR FRANCIS DRAKE SPECIAL
Courtesy, Hotel Sir Francis Drake, San Francisco

> ½ oz. gin
> ½ oz. bonded rye whisky
> ½ oz. Triple Sec
> ½ oz. green chartreuse

Stir well in mixing glass without ice. Serve in 2-oz. glass.

SLING

> 1 jigger liquor desired
> Lump sugar
> Nutmeg
> Teaspoon water
> Twist lemon peel

Use whichever liquor you prefer. A sling is served in a whisky glass. Dissolve sugar in water. Add liquor and lemon peel, grated nutmeg on top.

SLOE GIN RICKEY

> 1 jigger sloe gin
> Juice ½ lime and rind
> Cube ice

Place ice, lime juice and rind, and sloe gin in a Delmonico glass. Fill glass with club soda.

SMASH

1 jigger liquor
Few leaves mint
Teaspoon water
Lump sugar
Cube ice

This drink is a miniature Julep. Among the popular Smashes are Applejack, Bourbon, Brandy and Rye Smashes. A Smash is served in an old-fashioned glass. Muddle sugar, water, mint leaves in bottom of glass. Add liquor and ice. Stir.

SOHO

By Harry Craddock, The American Bar, The Dorchester, London

½ Chianti
¼ Italian vermouth
¼ grapefruit juice
Ice

Shake and serve in cocktail glass.

SONORA

By Harry Craddock, The American Bar, The Dorchester, London

½ tequila
½ pineapple juice
Dash grenadine
Ice

Shake and serve in cocktail glass.

SOURPUSS

1 jigger white Cuban rum
Juice ½ lime
1 teaspoon sugar
Ice

Shake. Strain into Delmonico glass. Put dash claret on top and half slice fresh lemon.

SOURS

1 jigger liquor desired
Juice ½ lemon
½ teaspoon sugar
Ice

Stir well and strain. All Sours are served in a Delmonico glass. Decorate with half slice orange and maraschino cherry.

The original Sour was a Bourbon or Rye Whisky Sour. During and after prohibition, many other Sours were originated.

SOUTH SIDE

Courtesy, The Colony Restaurant, New York City

1 jigger gin
½ teaspoon sugar
Juice ½ lime
Sprigs mint

Crush mint with sugar in mixing glass with muddler. Add ice and ingredients and shake well. Serve in parfait glass.

SPIRITS OF '76

Courtesy, The Carlyle, New York City

½ rum
¼ applejack
¼ papaya juice
Dash lemon juice
Ice

Serve in cocktail glass. This is a summer specialty.

SPRITZER

Rhine wine
Ice

In a highball glass, place ice and wine. Fill with club soda.

STAG LINES

By Bert Bacharach, Syndicated Columnist, Radio and TV Commentator

> 1 jigger Coronet brandy
> Dash Angostura bitters
> 2 dashes orgeat
> Ice
>
> *Shake well. Strain into cocktail glass, and add twist lemon peel.*

STARLIGHT ROOF GARDEN COOLER

As prepared at the new Waldorf-Astoria, New York City

> 1 jigger French vermouth
> Juice 1 lime
> Dash bitters on lump sugar
> Bottle ginger ale
>
> *Serve in Collins glass with ice.*

STEAMBOAT

Courtesy, Log Cabin Club, St. Louis

> 2 jiggers 16-year-old bourbon
> ¼ large orange
> ⅛ lemon
> 1 teaspoon sugar
>
> *Crush sugar, orange and lemon with large wooden muddler in toddy glass. Fill glass with very fine ice, add bourbon, and frappé until very cold.*

STERN'S SPORTS SPECIAL

By Bill Stern, Sports Commentator, National Broadcasting Company, New York City

> 1 jigger gin
> 1½ oz. canned pineapple juice
> 1 egg white
>
> *Shake well in cocktail shaker with ice, and serve in chilled glass.*

229 : *Cocktails and Mixed Drinks*

STINGER

⅔ cognac

⅓ white crème de menthe

Pour over shaved ice, and serve in cocktail glass.

STINGER FOR FOUR

By John Stevenson, Publisher, New York City

4 oz. French cognac, brandy or armagnac

2 oz. white crème de menthe

Pour over 3 inches of cracked ice in a blender. Place top on blender, then turn switch for agitating 15 seconds. Pour into cocktail, wine or champagne glasses, and serve while slightly frappéed.

STONEHENGE COLLINS

Courtesy, Stonehenge Inn, Ridgefield, Connecticut

3 oz. gin

Juice 1 lemon

1 teaspoon sugar

¼ oz. green mint

Shake, and serve with ice in a goblet. Decorate with sprig mint, slice lemon, and maraschino cherry.

STONEHENGE PUNCH

Courtesy, Stonehenge Inn, Ridgefield, Connecticut

½ jigger bonded bourbon

½ jigger Barbados rum

Juice 1 lime

1 teaspoon sugar

Shake, and pour over shaved ice in a goblet. Garnish with fresh fruits.

230 : *Bottoms Up*

STOP AND GO (after-dinner drink)
By Ted Saucier

½ jigger cognac
1 jigger kirschwasser
1 oz. grenadine
1 jigger shaved ice
Green mint liqueur
Maraschino cherry

*Fill hollow stem of champagne glass with green
mint, and place cherry at opening of stem so mint
does not run out. Put ingredients into electric
mixer. Pour ice and all into champagne glass
before ice has entirely melted.*

STORK CLUB FROST
Courtesy, The Stork Club, New York City

½ oz. Triple Sec
3 oz. orange juice
1 oz. curaçao
Shaved ice

Mix in electric mixer and serve in Collins glass.

STROMBOLI
"An old-fashioned on the rocks."

SUFFERING BAR STEWARD
Courtesy, Shepheard's Hotel, Cairo

⅓ gin
⅓ bourbon
⅓ lime juice
Dash Angostura bitters

*Put into medium-sized glass, ice, and fill with
ginger ale. Add fresh mint and slice orange.*

231 : *Cocktails and Mixed Drinks*

SUNDOWNER

Courtesy, H. M. Moolman, Director, Union of South Africa Government Information Office, New York City

"This cocktail is a favorite in South Africa and carries no legacy of sore heads. If there is one South African drink that deserves mention as a typically national drink, it is Van der Hum. This is a liqueur with an international reputation. It has a tangerine base and, if desired, can be taken mixed with good brandy."

2 parts South African brandy (Cape of Good Hope is available in the United States)
1 part Van der Hum liqueur
3 parts orange and lemon juices, mixed in the proportion of 5 orange to 1 lemon, or to taste

Add brandy and Van der Hum to juices, and shake with ice. Serve in cocktail glass.

SUN VALLEY SPICED WINE

Courtesy, Sun Valley Lodge, Sun Valley, Idaho

"This is quite a drink during the winter, being served at the Warming Huts and during tea hour in the village . . . a mild, heated ski drink sometimes called 'Glue Wine.'"

1 qt. claret
2 oranges, sliced with peel
2 lemons, sliced with peel
8 sticks cinnamon
12 cloves

Place ingredients in the wine while it is cold. Then heat wine to a point just below boiling, or steaming, and serve in a pottery wine mug.

SUPER CHIEF SPECIAL

Courtesy, Atchison, Topeka and Santa Fe Railway

1 jigger bourbon
2 dashes Angostura bitters

Put into old-fashioned glass filled with crushed ice. Serve with twisted lime peel.

SURF CLUB

Courtesy, The Surf Club, Miami Beach

"This drink is very popular with cabana parties as its color reflects the turquoise of the nearby Gulf Stream. It seems to blend particularly well into the picture."

½ dry gin
¼ kirschwasser
¼ lime juice
Dash blue vegetable extract
Ice

Shake well, and strain into cocktail glass.

SWEET SUMMER BREEZE

Courtesy, Billy Reed, The Little Club, New York City

1 jigger brandy
½ jigger Cointreau
2 cubes ice

Mix in highball glass. Add ice, and fill with champagne. Serve.

233 : *Cocktails and Mixed Drinks*

Into a crystal cup the dusky wine
I pour, and, musing at so rich a shrine,
I watch the star that haunts its ruddy gloom.

GEORGE STERLING
(*A Wine of Wizardry*)

TALENT SCOUT

By Arthur Godfrey, Radio and TV Commentator

2 jiggers Old Charter bourbon
Dash Grand Marnier liqueur
Dash Angostura bitters
Cracked ice

Shake and serve in old-fashioned glass with twist lemon peel.

TARA BROOCH

By Gerald McCann, Conductor "After Theater" Column, The Playbill

"The fragrance of the cucumber and that of the whisky have a particular affinity and the combination is as pleasant to smell as it is to taste."

2 oz. Irish whisky

Pour whisky into mixer with ice. Stir thoroughly. Cut a fairly thick slice of unpeeled cucumber and place it in the bottom of a chilled champagne glass. Pour in the liquor and sip.

TERRACE GRILL

Courtesy, Hotel Muehlebach, Kansas City

⅓ oz. Three-Star Hennessy
⅓ oz. apricot brandy
⅓ oz. gin
Ice

Shake well, and serve in cocktail glass.

THEODORE'S

Courtesy, Theodore's Restaurant, New York City

¾ jigger Schenley gin
¼ jigger Cherry Heering
Ice

Stir well. Strain into cocktail glass. Add twist lemon peel.

Tiger Lily

By ROBERT BUSHNELL

1 jigger Carioca rum
½ jigger Coronet brandy
½ jigger DuBouchett curaçao
Juice ½ lemon
Juice ¼ orange
Ice

Shake well. Strain over cracked ice into old-fashioned glass. Add twist lemon peel.

THIN MAN

In Honor of William Powell, Motion Picture Star

1 oz. dry gin
1 oz. curaçao
1 oz. heavy cream
Ice

Shake well, and strain into cocktail glass.

THIS IS NEW YORK

By Bill Leonard, Radio Commentator

⅔ jigger light Cuban rum
⅙ jigger fresh lime
⅙ jigger blackberry brandy
Ice

Shake well. Strain into cocktail glass.

THREE GRACES

By John La Gatta, Artist and Illustrator

1 jigger bourbon
Dash bitters
Sugar to taste
Sprig mint

Crush sugar and mint together. Add bourbon and enough ice to chill thoroughly. Serve in a cocktail glass. (Actually, this is a Mint Julep in cocktail form.)

TIGER SPECIAL

Courtesy, Princeton Club of New York

2 oz. light rum
½ oz. Cointreau
Juice ½ lime
Ice

Shake well, and strain into cocktail glass.

237 : *Cocktails and Mixed Drinks*

T.N.T.

By Tay Garnett, Motion Picture Director

1 jigger Schenley Reserve whisky
½ jigger Coronet brandy
½ jigger apricot brandy
Juice ¼ lemon
Ice

Shake well. Serve over cracked ice in old-fashioned glass. Add twist lemon peel.

TOAST OF THE TOWN

By Ed Sullivan, Author of the Column, "Little Old New York," New York Daily News, and TV Master of Ceremonies

⅔ jigger aged bourbon
⅓ jigger Italian vermouth
Ice

Shake well. Stain into cocktail glass. Decorate with maraschino cherry.

TODDY

1 jigger spirits desired
Lump sugar
3 teaspoons water

Generally hot water is used and other ingredients. Among the most popular Toddies are Applejack, Bourbon, Brandy, Gin, Rum and Rye Toddies. A Toddy is served in an old-fashioned glass. Put sugar in glass and dissolve in water. Add liquor, lump of ice, and dash of nutmeg. For a Hot Toddy, leave out the ice and add hot water.

TOM COLLINS

1 jigger Old Tom gin
½ barspoon powdered sugar
Juice ½ lemon

Shake well and strain into Collins glass. Add lump ice, and fill glass with soda water.

TONY VAUGHN

Courtesy, Hotel Jaragua, Ciudad Trujillo, Dominican Republic

1½ oz. rum Blanca
3 dashes benedictine
Dash Angostura
2 dashes dry and sweet vermouth
Ice

Stir. Serve in cocktail glass with orange peel.

TOP HAT TRIVIA

By Charles Ventura, Society Columnist, New York World-Telegram and Sun

1 jigger dry gin
1 teaspoon curaçao
1 teaspoon grenadine
Juice ½ lime
Shaved ice

Mix in electric mixer. Serve frappéed in champagne glass. Decorate with twist of fresh lime peel.

TOSCANINI

Courtesy, Hotel Astor, New York City

1 part Cordial Médoc
1 part cognac
1 part Cointreau
3 parts champagne

Serve in champagne glass with ice cube.

TOWN HOUSE

Courtesy, Zebra Room, The Town House, Los Angeles

⅔ white rum
⅓ pineapple and orange juice
2 or 3 dashes apricot brandy

Shake well with cracked ice, and strain into cocktail glass.

239 : *Cocktails and Mixed Drinks*

TRADER VIC

By Trader Vic, Trader Vic's Trading Post, Oakland, California

> 1½ oz. Siegert's Bouquet
> Juice ½ lime
> 1 teaspoon sugar
>
> *Squeeze lime into shaker. Add ice, rum and sugar. Shake and strain into chilled cocktail glass.*

TULANE

Courtesy, The Roosevelt, New Orleans

> ⅓ dry gin
> ⅓ French vermouth
> ⅓ strawberry brandy
>
> *Shake well with ice, and strain into cocktail glass.*

TUXEDO PARK

> ⅔ jigger dry gin
> ⅓ jigger dry sherry
> Dash orange bitters
> Ice
>
> *Stir. Strain into cocktail glass.*

TV BLUES

By Ben Gross, Radio and TV Editor, New York Daily News

> 1 jigger applejack
> Dash Cointreau
> Juice ½ lime
> Ice
>
> *Shake well, and serve in cocktail glass.*

TWENTY-ONE CLUB

Courtesy, Jack and Charlie's, New York City

> 4 parts "21" Club special whisky
> 1 part Tribuno sweet vermouth
> Ice
>
> *Stir well, and pour into cocktail glass. Squeeze orange peel over top for oil.*

TWO RUTHS

1 jigger light rum
Juice ½ lemon
½ jigger pineapple juice
½ jigger apricot brandy
Shaved ice

*Mix in electric mixer, and served frappéed in
cocktail glass.*

Wine that maketh glad the heart of man.

PSALM 104:15

UNION LEAGUE CLUB SPECIAL
Courtesy, The Union League Club, New York City

1½ oz. rye or bourbon
½ oz. Jamaica rum
½ oz. curaçao
½ oz. lemon juice
½ oz. orange juice
½ teaspoon powdered sugar
Ice

Shake well, and strain into 5-oz. goblet.

244 : *Bottoms Up*

What's drinking?
A mere pause from thinking!

GEORGE GORDON, LORD BYRON
(*The Deformed Transformed*)

VALOIS

Courtesy, Le Valois, New York City

1 jigger gin
Dash Cointreau
Juice ½ lime
Dash cherry brandy

Shake well with ice. Serve in cocktail glass.

VARIETY MARTINI

By Abel Green, Editor, Variety, New York City

3 parts Booth's House of Lords gin
1 part Martini & Rossi dry vermouth
Dash absinthe or absinthe substitute
Pearl onion
Lemon peel

Serve in cocktail glass with firm, imported Holland pearl onion and small piece of lemon peel. Add dash absinthe or absinthe substitute.

VERMOUTH OLD-FASHIONED

1½ oz. vermouth
Dash Angostura bitters
Cube sugar

Muddle sugar and bitters in old-fashioned glass with dash soda water. Add cracked ice, vermouth and twist lemon peel. Stir.

VIRGIN

½ jigger gin
½ jigger crème de menthe
½ jigger Forbidden Fruit
Ice

Shake well. Strain into cocktail glass. Decorate with maraschino cherry.

VODKA DAISY

1 jigger vodka
6 dashes grenadine
Juice ½ lemon
½ teaspoon powdered sugar

Half fill a highball glass with finely cracked ice. Stir until glass is frosted. Pour ingredients over ice. Fill with soda water. Decorate with sprig fresh mint, slice lemon and slice orange.

VODKA HIGHBALL

1 jigger vodka
Charged water
Cracked ice

A tall drink, served in a large highball glass. Pour vodka over ice, and fill with club soda or ginger ale, instead of charged water, if desired.

VODKA OLD-FASHIONED

1½ oz. vodka
Dash Angostura bitters
Cube sugar
Twist lemon peel

Place sugar, bitters and dash soda water in old-fashioned glass. Muddle. Add cracked ice, vodka, and lemon peel.

VODKA ON THE ROCKS

1 jigger vodka
Dash water or soda
Twist lemon peel
Cracked ice

Fill an old-fashioned glass with the ice. Pour in vodka, add water. Also lemon peel, if desired.

247 : *Cocktails and Mixed Drinks*

VODKA SOUR

1 jigger vodka
Juice ½ lemon
½ barspoon powdered sugar
Ice

*Shake well and strain into glass. Add dash siphon
or soda water, half slice orange, and cherry.*

VODKATINI
By Jerome Zerbe, Photographer, and Society Editor of Town and
Country

⅘ jigger Smirnoff vodka
⅕ jigger dry vermouth
Ice

*Stir in mixer. Strain into cocktail glass, and add
twist lemon peel.*

VOLCANO HOUSE HOT BUTTERED RUM
*By Bob A. Ida, Head Bartender, Volcano House, Hawaii National
Park*

"A welcome drink on cold rainy days."

1 jigger Myers' rum
½ jigger sirup
½ jigger lemon juice
Few dashes maraschino liqueur
Twist lemon peel

*Put into large-sized gin fizz glass. Fill rest of glass
with very hot tea. Stir well, then float small piece
of butter, and add 3 or 4 pieces of cloves.*

Give me a bowl of wine;
In this I bury all unkindness.

WILLIAM SHAKESPEARE
(Julius Caesar)

WAIKIKI

1 jigger gin
1 oz. orange juice
1 oz. pineapple juice
Dash lemon juice
Dash Angostura bitters
Powdered sugar
Ice

Shake and strain into cocktail glass. Serve with fresh pineapple stick.

WALDORF

As served at the old Waldorf-Astoria.

⅓ whisky
⅓ Italian vermouth
⅓ absinthe (or absinthe substitute)
Dash Abbott's bitters

Frappé.

WALDORF-ASTORIA (after-dinner drink)

As served at the old Waldorf-Astoria.

1 pony benedictine
Sweetened whipped cream
Shaved ice

Pour benedictine on shaved ice. Cover and build in mound with whipped cream.

WALDORF FIZZ

As prepared at the old Waldorf-Astoria.

1 jigger High & Dry gin
Juice 1 orange
Juice 1 lemon
1 egg
1 barspoon sugar
Ice

Shake, and strain into lemonade glass. Fill glass with siphon.

WALDORF FRAPPE

> 1 part Apricotine
> 1 part lime juice
>
> *Frappé. Serve in cocktail glass.*

WALDORF GLOOM LIFTER

As served at the old Waldorf-Astoria.

> 1 jigger Irish whisky
> ½ teaspoon Martell brandy
> 1 egg white
> Dash raspberry sirup
> Dash grenadine
> ½ teaspoon sugar
> Ice
>
> *Stir and strain into cocktail glass.*

WALDORF PUNCH

As concocted at the old Waldorf-Astoria.

> *Whisky with claret floated on top.*

WALTER WINCHELL FLASH

By Walter Winchell, Columnist, New York Daily Mirror, and International News Service, and Radio Commentator

> 1 jigger Coronet brandy
> Juice ½ lime
> 1 barspoon grenadine
> Cracked ice
>
> *Shake well, and strain into cocktail glass. Add twist orange peel.*

WARD EIGHT

> 1 jigger Schenley Reserve whisky
> Juice ½ lemon
> ½ teaspoon sugar
> 1 teaspoon grenadine
> Ice
>
> *Shake well, and strain into cocktail glass.*

WARDMAN PARK

Courtesy, Wardman Park Hotel, Washington, D. C.

1¼ oz. dry sherry
¾ oz. brandy
¾ oz. Drambuie

Stir well in ice, and strain into cocktail glass. Add lemon peel.

WASHINGTON STATLER

Courtesy, Hotel Statler Company, Inc., New York City

1½ oz. rum
½ oz. pineapple juice
3 dashes lime juice
3 dashes apricot cordial

Shake with chipped ice. Serve in cocktail glass.

WATTS' TODDY

Courtesy, Log Cabin Club, St. Louis

Bourbon whisky
Lemon peel
Ice (not cracked)

Fill toddy glass with ice. Add lemon peel. Pour good bourbon whisky into the crevices until glass is filled.

WEEK END AT THE WALDORF

Recalling the pleasant months spent by the author on the MGM lot during the filming of "Week End at the Waldorf."

1 jigger Carioca rum
Juice ½ lime
1 barspoon curaçao
1 barspoon strawberry sirup or cordial
Ice

Mix in electric mixer. Serve frappéed in cocktail glass.

WESTON SPECIAL
Courtesy, The Colony Restaurant, New York City

Dubonnet
2 slices lemon
Cracked ice

Fill water goblet with ice, then fill glass with Dubonnet. Decorate with lemon, and serve with long straw.

WESTPORT
By Bill Leonard, Commentator, Columbia Broadcasting System, New York City

⅔ white rum
⅙ blackberry brandy
⅙ lime juice

Serve with plenty of ice in cocktail glass.

WHISKY FIZZ

1 jigger rye whisky or bourbon
Juice ½ lemon
1 teaspoon sugar
Ice

Shake well, strain. Fill fizz glass with soda water.

WHISKY FLIP

1 jigger rye whisky or bourbon
½ teaspoon sugar
1 whole egg
Ice

Shake, strain. Pour into fizz glass. Grate nutmeg on top.

WHISKY SOUR RUM FLOAT
Courtesy, Noonday Club, St. Louis

1½ oz. bourbon
1 barspoon bar sirup
1 oz. lemon juice

Shake in cocktail shaker with ice. Strain into whisky sour glass. Garnish with slice orange and float a little Myers' rum on top.

253 : *Cocktails and Mixed Drinks*

WHITE LADY

⅓ gin
⅓ DuBouchett Cointreau
⅓ lemon juice
Ice

Shake well, and strain into cocktail glass.

WILKERSON DE LUXE
By Billy Wilkerson, Hollywood

1 oz. benedictine
1 oz. French vermouth
1 teaspoon absinthe
2 drops Angostura bitters

Mix in mixing glass. Serve in champagne glass with ice cube.

WILLARD HOTEL
Courtesy, The Willard, Washington, D. C.

⅓ apricot brandy
⅓ peach brandy
⅓ lime juice

Shake well in cracked ice, and serve in regular cocktail glass.

WILSON SPECIAL MARTINI
Courtesy, Beau Sejour, Bethpage, Long Island

2 oz. fine imported gin
⅓ teaspoon Italian vermouth
Drop absinthe

Shake short and vigorously. Strain and serve in cocktail glass. This should have the pale color of a regular dry Martini.

WINDSOR (formerly the Wally Simpson)

Courtesy, Arnaud's Restaurant, New Orleans

⅓ cognac
⅓ Italian vermouth
⅓ French vermouth
1 teaspoon lime juice
No sugar

Strain ingredients into champagne glass halfway. Fill glass with burgundy. Add few drops orange bitters, and drop in piece orange peel.

WINDSOR HOTEL

Courtesy, The Embassy Club, The Windsor Hotel, Montreal

1¼ oz. dry gin
¾ oz. green crème de menthe
Ice

Shake well, and strain into cocktail glass. Decorate with twist lemon peel.

WINDY CITY

By Nate Gross, Columnist, Chicago Herald-American

1 jigger Schenley gin
½ jigger DuBouchett Triple Sec
Juice ¼ lemon
Juice ¼ orange
Ice

Shake well. Serve in old-fashioned glass over cracked ice. Decorate with half slice orange.

WONDER BAR

Courtesy, Detroit Wonder Bar, Detroit

⅓ gin
⅓ Cointreau
⅓ pineapple juice

Shake well with cracked ice. Serve in cocktail glass.

WONDER BAR TOM AND JERRY

Courtesy, Detroit Wonder Bar, Detroit
A hot drink for a cold night.

> 12 eggs
> Powdered sugar
> ½ jigger rum
> ½ jigger brandy
> Hot water
> Nutmeg

Separate eggs. Mold sugar into yolks until so stiff it will not take any more sugar. Beat whites until stiff. Then put whites on yolks and mix slowly until batter forms. Portions are 1 teaspoon batter to ½ jigger rum and ½ jigger brandy. Serve in mug. Add hot water and nutmeg.

256 : *Bottoms Up*

Fill every beaker up, my men, pour forth
    the cheering wine:
There's life and strength in every drop,
    —thanksgiving to the vine!

ALBERT GORTON GREENE
(The Baron's Last Banquet)

YALE

½ jigger dry gin
½ jigger Italian vermouth
Dash orange bitters

*Pour over cracked ice in Delmonico glass. Stir.
Dash club soda on top.*

YALE CLUB MARTINI

*Courtesy, John S. Davidson, Secretary, The Yale Club,
New York City*

2 jiggers dry gin
¼ jigger imported French vermouth
Ice

*Stir. Strain into large 5-oz. cocktail glass or cham-
pagne saucer glass which has been previously
chilled. Add twist lemon peel.*

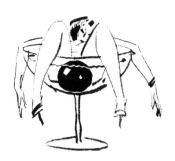

Oh, the clink of cups together,
With the daylight coming on!

RICHARD HOVEY
(*Comrades*)

ZAZA

> 1 jigger dry gin
> 1 jigger Dubonnet
> Ice
>
> *Shake well. Strain into cocktail glass.*

ZOMBIE

Courtesy, Fairmont Hotel, San Francisco

> 1 oz. white rum
> ½ oz. dark rum
> ½ oz. 151-proof rum
> 1 oz. Passion Fruit
> ½ oz. pineapple juice
> 1 oz. lime juice
>
> *Blend in electric mixer. Serve in 14-oz. highball glass, to which has been added shaved ice. Decorate with slice fresh lemon, slice fresh lime, maraschino cherry.*

Au Revoir

La vie est vaine:
* Un peu d'amour,*
Un peu de haine. . . .
* Et puis—Bon jour!*

La vie est brève:
* Un peu d'espoir,*
Un peu de rêve
* Et puis—Bon soir!*

LEON MONTENAEKEN
(*Peu de Chose*)

(*Translation*)

Ah, brief is Life,
  Love's short sweet way,
With dreamings rife,
  And then—Good day!

And Life is vain—
  Hope's vague delight,
Grief's transient pain,
  And then—Good night!

LOUISE CHANDLER MOULTON

Index

266 : *Index*

CPSIA information can be obtained
at www.ICGtesting.com
Printed in the USA
BVHW020438181222
654236BV00003B/60

9 781891 396656